WE WERE THERE

DEDICATION

This is
for my mother

MARY A. WEBER

small in size
but large in spirit and dreams

We Were There

Women in the New Testament

LUCY FUCHS

ALBA·HOUSE   alba house   NEW·YORK

SOCIETY OF ST. PAUL, 2187 VICTORY BLVD., STATEN ISLAND, NEW YORK 10314

Library of Congress Cataloging-in-Publication Data

Fuchs, Lucy.
    We were there : women in the New Testament / by Lucy Fuchs.
        p.   cm.
    ISBN 0-8189-0648-0
    1. Women in the Bible.   2. Bible.   N.T. — Study and teaching.
  I.   Title.
  BS2445.F83   1993   93-24987
  225.9'22'082 — dc20   CIP

Produced and bound in the United States of America
by the Fathers and Brothers of the
Society of St. Paul, 2187 Victory Boulevard,
Staten Island, New York 10314, as part of their
communications apostolate.

PRINTING INFORMATION:

Current Printing - first digit 1 2 3 4 5 6 7 8 9 10 11 12

Year of Current Printing - first year shown

   1993   1994   1995   1996   1997   1998   1999 2000

Table of Contents

Introduction

This series of meditations and discussions on women in the New Testament grew out of monthly Bible discussions which were held with the women in leadership in our parish. I was asked to give them some thoughts which would make the Scriptures come alive, along with some questions for discussion. I was delighted to be asked.

As I studied the Scriptures, reading the passages many times, praying over them, and searching in commentaries, I began to see a pattern. Jesus liked women! He never once treated a woman as anything less than an important person, worthy of respect. Very frequently he seemed to find women even more responsive to his message than men. When he needed some rest he would go to Bethany where he knew that Martha and Mary would welcome him. Women were with him throughout his life and women were with him at death. After his death, when he rose again gloriously, women were the first to be granted the privilege of seeing him. No wonder Christianity has always appealed to women.

These meditations are certainly not limited to women's groups, but perhaps they will be most useful there. They are not meant to take the place of reading the Scriptures themselves. Nothing can ever do that. Instead, after the members of a group, or an individual alone, have read the selections in the New Testament, the words of the meditation should be read and thought about or discussed. I have

included some discussion questions which may prove
useful.

My intention in writing these meditations was to share
with readers what I have learned from my study of the Bible.
Perhaps they will have far different insights than mine as
they do their own study. That would please me very much.
After all, Jesus himself treated each person he met in a
unique way, responsive to his or her own needs.

Women in the Ancestry of Jesus
Matthew 1:1-16

ON the very first page of the New Testament, in the first chapter of the Gospel according to Matthew, we are given a list of some of the ancestors of Jesus. Matthew, writing for the Jews who knew the Old Testament, thought it important to give such a list. It was his purpose to show that Jesus was the promised Messiah. It was known that the Messiah was to come from the house and family of David, and by giving this list, Matthew shows Jesus to be descended from David.

Some of the names on the list are more familiar to us than others. To the Jews, it must have been an impressive list and served the purpose Matthew had in mind.

It is interesting to note that this list is prepared as the ancestry of Joseph, Mary's husband. We know, and Matthew makes it very clear, that Joseph was not the natural father of Jesus. Yet the ancestry was traced on his side.

Mary was also of the house of David, but it was not customary to trace lineage on the woman's side among the Jews, as was done in some other cultures. Although the Hebrew culture was, to a large extent, patriarchal, women were by no means ignored, and their influence was remembered. The women on Matthew's list were highly significant in Jesus' ancestry and mentioned for that reason.

Tamar, whose story is told in Genesis 38, was a widow of Judah's son. She felt ill-used by her husband's family and deprived of a child. However, she had no intention of allowing herself to continue to be deprived. Through trickery and deceit of her father-in-law, she became the mother of twin sons. Because of her action she barely escaped with her life. Few would consider her a great model of feminine behavior, but God saw fit to choose her son to carry on the lineage which would lead to Jesus.

Rahab, like Tamar, was not especially respectable. Her story is told in the book of Joshua. She was the harlot who saved the Israelite spies, and in return her whole family was saved from destruction. She was a foreigner, but because of her help, she was accepted as belonging to the Israelites.

Ruth too was a foreigner. She was a Moabite, married to a Jew, the son of Naomi. After the death of her husband, she went with her mother-in-law back to Bethlehem, where she met and married Boaz, and become an ancestor of Jesus.

Uriah's wife is mentioned on the list, although not by name. She is Bathsheba and her story is told in 2 Samuel 11. David desired the beautiful Bathsheba and to have her, he had Uriah killed. The child conceived in adultery died, but later David repented, and a second child grew to adulthood. This was the famous Solomon, widely known for his wisdom in ruling Israel.

Ruth is usually praised as an example of a devout and loyal woman, but Tamar, Rahab, and Bathsheba are not likely to be so praised.

In contrast to these women, there is Mary, the only other woman mentioned, and she is the glorious and untainted example of womanhood.

God makes use of all kinds of people to work his ways. They are often not the people we would choose. But God's ways are not our ways. St. Augustine was right: God can draw straight with crooked lines.

Jesus was born into a family which had its share of sin and strife. He counted in his ancestry great heroes, others who were not outstanding in any way, and still others whose lives were much less than edifying.

We too are born in those circumstances. What God is telling us is that it doesn't matter who our ancestors are, compared to his relationship to us.

The women in Matthew's list of Jesus' ancestry, with the exception of Mary, were unusual because they were, in a way, the non-legitimate members of the family. They were not the first or perhaps the legal wives, or, they were not native Israelites. And we are aware of the prejudices that existed between Israelites and other.

We cannot choose our relatives the way we choose our friends. When we are born, they are there. After we are gone, they will still be around. Sometimes we may wish that we had different relatives. But even Christ had some relatives that a devout Jew would not have been proud of.

DISCUSSION:

1. *Does it seem surprising that Jesus' ancestry included some disreputable characters along with some real saints? Does this make him more like us?*

2. *The only women mentioned in the list are those whose lives were unusual or irregular. Obviously there were many other women in Jesus' ancestry, but they were not mentioned because they were apparently good, devout women, who were dutiful and loving. Is there a message here?*

3. *We need relatives. At times they may drive us to distraction,
   but they constitute an important support group for most
   people. What can we say about the way families today are
   losing sight of close kinship relations?*

Mary at the Annunciation
Luke 1:26-38

LET us go to Nazareth today and learn about Mary. Nazareth was an unimportant town in Israel in those days and Mary was a small town girl living there. There is no evidence that there was anything obviously extraordinary about Mary before the Annunciation. We know, by our faith, that already the workings of God were marvelous within her, but nothing has come down to us of how she appeared to her fellow townspeople. She must have lived the simple life that all young women like her did. For the most part, she spent her time in domestic chores, the cooking, the weaving, the care of the household. Tradition has given us her mother's name, Anna, but we really know little of her life in those years.

Scholars tell us that Mary was probably only about fifteen when the angel Gabriel came with the strange and miraculous message. In just a few lines the Scriptures tell us that God sent the angel because he had a message for Mary. Gabriel greeted her: "Peace be with you! The Lord is with you!"

Her first reaction was one of wonderment. What did this message mean?

Gabriel went on to assure her: "Do not be afraid."

The message of God is always one which speaks of peace and takes away fear. It is God himself who will guide you, Gabriel said, fear not.

Then Gabriel went on to give the message to Mary, how she would become pregnant and bear a son whom she must name Jesus, one who will be called the son of the Most High God.

When we read this it is all so clear to us. Not only have we read it a thousand times, but we have also heard all of the theological interpretations of it, all the expounding of the meaning and manner of the Incarnation.

But it was not all that clear to this young girl. We do not even know whether she understood "Son of God" in its truest sense. In those days many people were called sons of God. What is clear to us is her profound act of faith here.

She believed that whatever Gabriel foretold would come to pass. She believed. But she did not understand how, and she asked, "I am a virgin. How, then, can this be?"

It would be through the power of God, the angel told her, the Holy Spirit would act upon her. And nothing is impossible with God.

Mary believed and accepted. The message was one of great joy. That she would bear a great son was certainly a message that any woman would be pleased to hear. And this son would be more than great. He would be God himself. That is more than we can truly contemplate.

Mary's attitude is one of acceptance. It would not be long before problems would arise. Joseph whom she loved would wonder about her, until he too would be enlightened by an angel. There would be the problems of being far from home at the time of Jesus' birth. There would be the flight into Egypt and the fear that her child would be killed. And later, she did in fact watch as he was put to death.

Now she knew none of those things. All she knew was that if God spoke to her and asked something of her, she would accept. And he would take care of her.

Mary's faith was, like ours must be, a leap into the dark. We never know what will happen in our own lives when we accept what God asks of us. And he does speak to us. Most likely, he does not speak to us through an angel like Gabriel. But he does speak to us in the depths of our souls. At times he speaks to us through our neighbor, requesting something of us. When we, like Mary, believe in his message and accept whatever he asks, he too will guide us.

DISCUSSION:

1. *What do you think Mary would be like if you met her on a street in Nazareth before the visit from Gabriel? After the visit?*

2. *We do not usually receive visits from angels, but God does speak to us and ask things of us. In what ways does God speak to us? How do we know when messages are from God?*

3. *Mary, like us, could not possibly know all that would happen in her life and the life of her son. Certainly, however, she must have known that from the moment of the message on, her life would not be an ordinary one. What does this suggest to us of trusting God to lead our way through the years ahead? Would we want to know the future if we could?*

Joseph's Response to Mary's Pregnancy

Matthew 1:18-21

JOSEPH and Mary were engaged to be married, the marriage having been arranged by their relatives, as was customary in the times. However, it is very likely that they knew each other long before their betrothal. Nazareth was small enough that families knew each other. Already probably many persons in the village were predicting that these two young people would be ideally suited to each other. How right they were would soon be evident.

When we think of arranged marriages, we tend to compare them with the so-called love marriages of today and see them as less desirable. But people in those times took a different view. A marriage was then, as it still is today, more than just an agreement between two people. It involved the whole family and all the relatives. Thus, everyone was concerned about making a good match.

Mary and Joseph too were part of this custom. Their families, about which we know very little except that they were both of the house of David (no doubt one important element in their marriage arrangement), decided that these two were suited to one another. An arranged marriage did not mean that the wishes of the young persons were totally ignored, just that they weren't the most important consideration. People did not expect to be in love before they were married. Rather, they saw love as one of the results of the marriage.

In any case, Joseph comes across as a fine young man. Mary would have been only about fifteen years old at this time, and Joseph was perhaps eighteen. He had a trade, we know, that of a carpenter.

The betrothal ceremony was one of great formality, almost as important as the wedding ceremony itself. The young persons made a solemn promise to each other to marry. They were no longer free to consider other suitors.

The betrothal period gave the young couple an opportunity to get to know each other better. From what we have seen, Mary and Joseph apparently saw each other frequently. But they still did not share their intimate thoughts. Mary did not tell him her most tremendous news. Indeed, one wonders how she could possibly have told him that.

Yet Joseph was watching her and he was deeply troubled, for it became clear that Mary was pregnant. We can imagine how he must have felt. He thought he knew what manner of woman Mary was, but the evidence was before his eyes. What could he do?

Joseph, the Bible tells us, was a just man. He knew his obligations to the Jewish law. Infidelity during the time of betrothal was equivalent to adultery. But Joseph could not bring himself to punish Mary. He searched for a way out. Maybe he could just privately put her aside, break the engagement.

How painful this must have been for Joseph, because by now, he must have loved her. And then he had a dream.

An angel told him not to fear. The child to be born of Mary was conceived by the Holy Spirit. He should take Mary as his wife. Mary needed him, as the child would need him. This child was to be called Jesus for he would be a savior.

Joseph must have woke up that morning with a deep peace. God would guide him. And now he could look at

Mary again with love and trust. His perceptions of her had been right. Mary was exactly what he thought of her and more — a beautiful and sinless young woman.

There is no evidence in the Scriptures that after this dream Joseph went to Mary and said to her, "I know your secret." But probably that was not necessary. The next time Joseph and Mary saw each other, a simple look might have told it all. With two people this close to God, surely there must have been deep understanding between them.

How Mary must have suffered during these days too. If even the one who loved her most, Joseph, wondered about her, what must the townspeople have thought. Yet Mary could not explain to them. She had to bear in silence the wonderful and strange things that were happening to her. One side of her must have been filled with joy that God was acting in her. The other must have been tinged with sorrow at the misunderstandings caused to others.

We all have experiences like these on a lesser level. At times we know that others, even those who love us, do not understand what we are doing. Then we, like Mary, must place our trust in God. He will guide both us and those whom we love.

DISCUSSION:

1. *Because of the painful experience of misunderstanding related in this story, Joseph and Mary were no doubt drawn closer to each other. Does this happen sometimes in our own lives? Can misunderstandings draw us together as well as divide us?*

2. *Notice that God did not enlighten Joseph until after he had suffered and questioned. Why does God seem to wait sometimes until the last minute?*

3. *Mary was given a most marvelous gift from God, but it required great faith and some suffering. Is this true of all of God's gifts?*

Mary Visits Elizabeth

Luke 1:39-45

THIS is a very womanly story — two women relating to each other. In fact, as far as I know this is the only incident in the Gospel which is entirely between women. In most Gospel stories women were relating to men, or men are relating to men. Here we have two women relating to each other.

Both of these women are worth looking much closer at. Mary, of course, has been looked at so often we hardly see her any more. In other places in these meditations we look at her again.

Here let us look at Elizabeth, the mother of John the Baptist. As we know she was a woman saddened by the fact that she had had no children. In Luke 1:5-7 we are told: "During the time when Herod was king of Judea, there was a priest named Zechariah, who belonged to the priestly order of Abiah. His wife's name was Elizabeth; she also belonged to a priestly family. They both lived good lives in God's sight, and obeyed fully all the Lord's commandments and rules. They had no children because Elizabeth could not have any, and she and Zechariah were both very old."

How old were they? Maybe only about 50. But the story is clear that she is unlikely to have children. In those days, to be childless was to be considered not in the good graces of God. Children were considered a blessing and the woman who had no children saw herself as somehow less than a woman. It was a public disgrace.

In fact, people were likely to claim that she must have been guilty of sin. However, in this story we are told clearly that she was a woman who lived a good life and obeyed all of God's commandments.

By now, as she was getting old, maybe into menopause or beyond it, she might have become resigned to the childless life she and Zechariah lived. There would be no child for her. She could not understand the strange ways of God.

Then her husband had that strange vision in the temple. The angel Gabriel had appeared to him and told him that he would be the father of a great son. And he doubted the angel. Because of his doubt, he was struck dumb.

We can imagine what it was like for Elizabeth. The whole village was no doubt talking about the strange events in the temple. Zechariah had come out unable to speak, but he had made it clear that he had a vision. Everyone knew that when God spoke to people, it was always a life-changing experience.

That was the kind of experience it was for Elizabeth too. For very soon after Zechariah returned home, she found herself pregnant. She, who was so sure that she would never have children. How happy she was to await her child. "Now at last the Lord had helped me in this way," she said, "He has taken away my public disgrace!"

But she must have had many misgivings. What child would this be, she thought, given to her late in life and heralded by an angel. She may have stayed at home for five months, not leaving the house unless absolutely necessary.

Part of this was, no doubt, her natural concern of caring for this child in her womb. But part of it was also the feeling she must have had that things beyond human understanding were happening here. She must not be the object of gossip and speculation.

Zechariah was not the only one who was having visions. Over in Nazareth, Elizabeth's much younger cousin Mary also had a vision. We know that Mary was probably only about fifteen years old. She was receiving the most stupendous message ever given to a human being. It would not only affect her life, but the life of the whole human race until the end of time.

In the midst of this message, Gabriel told Mary a bit of news: "Remember your relative Elizabeth. It is said that she cannot have children; but she herself is now six months pregnant, even though she is very old. For there is not a thing that God cannot do" (Luke 1:36-37).

When the angel left, leaving Mary with the incredible understanding that God had visited the human race in visiting her, she felt the need to confide in someone.

Interestingly enough, she does not go to Joseph, even though she is betrothed to him. Apparently women did not talk about such intimate things to their men. And we know that her not telling Joseph was the cause of great anguish to him.

Instead Mary goes to see the one person whom she knows will understand. Mary was the kind of person who would think of Elizabeth's needs. Maybe she needed help. A woman her age might have a very difficult pregnancy.

And so, she traveled to see Elizabeth. There was a distance here of perhaps ninety miles. She would have walked, but she would not have gone alone. Perhaps there was a caravan going that way and she could go along. We do not know all the details. We do not know if her mother went with her either. But apparently she went as soon as possible.

She could not wait to see Elizabeth. And when she did see her, she did not even have to tell her what had happened to her. She greeted Elizabeth and as soon as Elizabeth heard the greeting, she also felt a movement of her son within her womb. This was probably the first time she had felt him. This was perhaps what they used to call "the quickening," the time when a woman feels the movement of life within her. Elizabeth was filled with the Holy Spirit. The Holy Spirit himself told her what was happening to Mary. Her response to Mary was one of joy and humility.

This was an amazing response. The people of those days were much aware of age deference. Here the older woman praises the younger woman and tells how undeserving she is that such a woman should come to see her.

Mary's response is a praising of God. She will take no credit for herself. Mary will express her wonderment too at the strange working of God.

Thus we have two women, cousins, far different in age, but both full of the Spirit of God.

It is an old myth that women cannot get along, that they are always back-biting and envious of each other. This is the only story of two women relating to each other without the presence of men in the New Testament, and their attitude toward each other is one of joy and praise of God. They are women to whom God has done marvelous things and they will praise him for it. They will not compare their wonders. Instead they are in awe of the ways of God with them.

Then what did Mary do? Luke 1:56 tells us that "Mary stayed about three months with Elizabeth and then went back home."

No doubt she helped her work. There was and still is always work for women to do, the cooking, the weaving, the spinning, the care of the house. And as they worked no doubt the two women enjoyed each other's company, knowing that they had each found someone who could share their deepest feelings.

DISCUSSION:

1. *What can we learn from this story about a woman support system in which women help each other? Have we found this to be true in our lives?*
2. *What comments could you make about the fact that Mary did not tell Joseph her marvelous news?*
3. *Does this story teach us anything about relationships between older and younger women?*

Mary at Bethlehem
Luke 2:1-20

THIS is the simplest, yet perhaps the most profound story in all the Bible. A woman gives birth to a son. What could be more simple than that?

But what a child, and what a birth!

We know how Joseph, because he was of the house and family of David, went to Bethlehem, and how Mary went with him. Mary was in the last days of her pregnancy. The trip could not have been easy for her. Yet she, who accepted at the Annunciation all that God had said, would accept this too. She knew well that there was a reason for her to be in Bethlehem for the birth of her child.

We also know how there was no room for them at the inn, and so they found a stable and placed him in a manger. Jesus was not born in luxury and in pomp. This is of great significance. Think what it would have been like if Mary and Joseph had been wealthy rulers and Jesus had been born in a palace. What a loss this would have been for all the poor people of the world. The world always seems to belong to the wealthy few, while the millions of poor are left out. Yet God loves them, and here he chose that his Son was to be born poor, to identify with them.

But it is unlikely that being rich or poor ever went through Mary's mind when her child was born. In this she was like all mothers. She could think of nothing but her new son and the great joy she felt with him. She must have held him in her arms and just looked at him.

All births of sons among the Jews were causes of great joy, but this was exceptional. Apparently, however, for a little while, there was no one to share the joy with. Mary and Joseph just looked at Jesus and at one another and glowed with joy.

But they were not alone for long. Out on the hillside, shepherds were watching their sheep. How fitting this is. Bethlehem was where King David had been born, which was why Joseph went there for the census. David had started out as a simple shepherd, known only for his extreme care in protecting his sheep. Now, centuries later, shepherds were still in the area.

The shepherd's life was not an easy one. He was expected to stay out with the sheep through good weather and bad, and on some nights the wind and the rain were exceedingly cold. Yet he could not desert his sheep. Some shepherds, like David, apparently spent their long lonely hours composing poetry. Others simply endured. But they all loved their sheep and knew them well. Later Jesus would use the image of the Good Shepherd when describing himself, and the people would understand.

Now the joy of the birth of this Divine Son was too much to be contained in one man and one woman in a small stable. The joy had to be shared. And so God sent an angel to the shepherds to tell them the good news.

We can imagine this scene. The shepherds were standing, ever alert, with their sheep, when suddenly the entire sky grew bright as the glory of the Lord shone over them. They were frightened, as we can well believe. But the angel told them the same thing that an angel had told Mary, "Do not be afraid!"

He went on to tell them the good news. Jesus was born in the city of David, he would be the savior and bring joy to all the people. And the angel told them how they would recognize him. He would be wrapped in swaddling clothes and lying in a manger.

Then the sky was filled with angels all singing praises to God. The shepherds could do nothing else but obey. They went off immediately and found the Holy Family with the baby lying in the manger. How Mary and Joseph must have been surprised to see these shepherds arriving in the middle of the night, hesitating perhaps, yet persistent, and wanting to see the baby.

The shepherds told Mary and Joseph what they had seen and heard. Mary must have been happy to share her joy. Every woman thinks she has the most wonderful baby in the world. Here even the angels were attesting to it.

Mary remembered all these things and thought deeply about them. She would never forget a single detail of the birth of her son. How could she? He was all of her life.

This story is close to the heart of Mary's life, of every

woman's life. It cannot be said that a woman is incomplete unless she has a child. Yet, many women attest to the fact that bearing a child is the most fulfilling event in their lives. All women, whether they have children of their own or not, share in the need to give and share life. This marvelous desire to pass on life, this joy in the caring of the little, the weak, and the helpless, this is a great gift that brings us close to God, the giver of all life.

DISCUSSION:

1. *How do you think Mary felt when she arrived in Bethlehem and found no room at the inn, just at the time when a place was most needed? How would you have felt?*

2. *Does the fact that Jesus chose to be born poor make a difference in the world today? What does it mean to be poor?*

3. *Whatever other title we give Mary, the most important one will always be Mother. Is there any way in which all women can identify with this?*

Mary at the Coming of the Wise Men

Matthew 2:1-12

JESUS was born, and his coming could not be contained in the small town of Bethlehem. It needed to be heralded to the world.

We can imagine Mary at the birth of Jesus. We know what mothers are like when children are born. Their whole world is right in their arms with the child. Mary must have held Jesus to her heart and rocked and sang to him. Her joy was full. Yet even with the joy were many wonderings. What would his future be?

His beginnings were most extraordinary. Just a short time ago, Mary had been only a simple small town girl going about her daily tasks. She had been betrothed to Joseph, a fine young man whom she had learned to love. But an angel had come and changed her life forever.

And now she was holding a baby who was the Son of God himself. Mary knew very well that his life — and hers — would be extraordinary. But just how things would develop she had no way of knowing. The angel Gabriel had said very little. Mary had believed his message and accepted God's will, and she would take each day as it came.

Now there was a noise from outside. She could hear the sound of many voices and a sense of excitement in the air. Perhaps Joseph went to look at what was going on. He peered out and saw a group of strangers, clearly from the East, wearing exotic-looking clothing. It was also clear that these men were wealthy. They may have been riding camels and were certainly surrounded by servants.

As Joseph looked on in astonishment, they came right to the place where he and Mary were. They dismounted their camels and moved forward respectfully, as they would approach a king.

"There is a child here, a new-born son, is there not?" Perhaps one of them asked in faltering language.

Joseph nodded. "Why yes," he may have stammered.

"May we see him?" they asked with great reverence.

Again Joseph nodded and stepped aside.

They entered slowly and respectfully, and fell down before the child, worshipping him.

Mary held Jesus in her arms, presenting him to these visitors. She understood why these men were worshipping her child. And yet, her mother's heart was urging, "He is still a very tiny baby. Am I to give him up to the world so soon?"

Later the wise men must have told Mary and Joseph their story. They were astrologers from the East. They had spent their lives studying the stars. A new star had appeared in the sky and they knew that meant the arrival of a new king. They could only search until they found him. They had followed the star for many nights. They rested during the days, looking forward eagerly to the dark so that they could take up their route again. But when they had arrived in Jerusalem they did not know where to go. So they had gone to the palace of Herod the king.

Mary and Joseph nodded. Of course, when searching for a king a palace would be a logical place to go. But already Mary was becoming fearful. She and Joseph knew what the wise men did not know, that Herod was a dangerous man. He would be most upset by the thought of any king coming to challenge his rule.

Yet Herod had helped the wise men. He had called together the chief priests and the Jewish wise men and asked them where the Messiah was to be born. They came back with the message: the Messiah was to be born in Bethlehem.

Ah, Bethlehem, Herod thought. And so he called the wise men, "Go and find him and then come and tell me where he is. I too want to go and worship him."

They left his presence and immediately, as soon as it got dark that night, they saw the star, brighter than ever. It was right over a certain part of Bethlehem. Now they knew exactly where to go.

Mary and Joseph listened intently to this story. Clearly it was God's workings. They had never doubted his guidance before, and they would not doubt it now. But with Herod's knowledge of Jesus' birth there was bound to be trouble.

The wise men offered gifts to Jesus, gold, frankincense, and myrrh, costly and symbolic gifts.

Then the wise men were gone. Mary still held the baby in her arms. She must have looked at him and wondered. This child was already attracted visitors from afar and aroused jealousy in a king, yet he was a helpless baby who depended on Mary for all his needs.

It is thought-provoking to imagine the contemplation of Mary these days. She must have wanted at times to simply enjoy Jesus' presence and the joy he brought to her life as babies do, without contemplating the future. But the strange events that went on around her prevented that.

Other women do not give birth to such a son. Yet no woman ever knows all that may happen in the life of her child. The future is hidden from us all. When children are small, we can do no more than cherish them. As with Mary, however, they are never ours alone. No child ever belongs to the parents. They are simply lent to them for a while. Mary must have felt this very deeply in those first few days of his birth, especially at the time of these strange visitors.

DISCUSSION:

1. *It is easy to think of Mary in the light of what we know later of the life of Jesus. We must remember that at the birth of Jesus, Mary knew very little. Gabriel's message was very short. How does this give us Mary as an example of faith and trust in God?*

2. *What do you imagine Mary and Joseph said to each other after the wise men departed? What would they have done with the gifts that were offered?*

3. *Think about Mary's hopes and fears for Jesus. What do you imagine went through her mind?*

Mary's Flight into Egypt
Matthew 2:13-18

WE do not know how long the strange visitors from the East, the wise men searching for the new king, stayed in Bethlehem. After having come so far, they would not have left immediately.

Back in Jerusalem, Herod was upset at the thought of a new king. He had told the wise men to come back and tell him after they found the king. He wanted to worship him too, he said. He must have laughed to himself, thinking how they would do his work for him, finding the king.

But God would protect his own Son. In Bethlehem, Mary held him in her gentle arms and cared for him the way all mothers do, trusting in God's protection. When the wise men told her and Joseph of their meeting with King Herod in Jerusalem, they wondered. They knew Herod's reputation.

Then, as the wise men made preparation to leave Bethlehem, they had a dream. In it, God warned them about Herod. They must not go back to him. He wanted to kill the child.

They awoke, much sobered. They had come to believe in this child. They could not permit him to be harmed. And so they mapped out another route for their return. Herod would not see them again.

After they left, Bethlehem must have settled down again to its quiet ways. In their small house, Mary and Joseph spent their time caring for the baby, enjoying his presence. But perhaps they both sensed a foreboding.

Then Joseph had a dream in which an angel spoke to him, "Joseph, get up. Take the child and his mother and go to Egypt. Stay until I tell you to return. Herod will be looking for the child to kill him."

Joseph awoke, very disturbed. He must have looked at his sleeping wife and the beautiful sleeping child and hated to wake them. But he knew he must. They had few belongings. It could not have taken them long to get ready. But what a journey it would have been, all the way to Egypt.

At other times in Jewish history, people had fled into Egypt. Joseph knew well this history. His own patron Joseph, the son of Jacob, had been sold into Egypt, where he had eventually become important in the kingdom. But Egypt was never anything other than a land of exile. One of the strongest motifs among the Jews was the remembrance of their deliverance from Egypt on the night of the Passover. And now, Joseph and Mary would have to go there in order to save their child.

They went. They must have found the way long and hard. Most of the time they walked. Mary and Joseph probably took turns carrying the baby. They must have been weary many times. It was a long journey and the trip would have been doubly hard as they had had to make hurried plans to go.

Back in Jerusalem, Herod realized that he had

been tricked, that the wise men were not returning. He was furious. Somewhere out there was a baby boy who would grow up to be a king. Herod could not permit that. He gave orders to kill all the baby boys in Bethlehem, two years and younger. What a horrible sentence to have been passed on innocent children, and what a useless one. For the king had escaped Herod. And how little Herod understood of the ways of God. The new king would be a king forever over the minds and hearts of the world, but he did not wish an earthly throne.

In Egypt, it is unlikely that Mary and Joseph heard of Herod's massacre. All they knew was that God had sent them to Egypt for the protection of his Son. And for that they were truly grateful.

Yet it must have been difficult living in Egypt. This was a pagan country, with idol worship all around them. Even though many Jews lived in Egypt, Mary and Joseph felt themselves aliens, strangers in a strange land. On Mary's part, she must have often thought back to the day when Gabriel had come. She had accepted God's will then and she still accepted it, however strange it might be.

We do not know how long Mary, Joseph, and Jesus remained in Egypt. It may have been a few years. We know Joseph was a skilled carpenter, and no doubt he could find work. Mary would have stayed at home with Jesus, caring for him, watching him grow. Soon he was crawling, then standing, then learning to walk. His speech changed from cooing to words. The baby was growing up. He was God's own Son, but he was living in exile away from God's own land. No wonder we are often told in the Scriptures that Mary cherished all these things in her heart.

DISCUSSION:

1. *Wherever women go, they make a home. This need is especially strong when there are children. Mothers want to provide a comfortable and secure place for their children. How do you picture Mary in Egypt trying to make a home for Jesus and Joseph?*

2. *Mary had to watch Jesus growing up in the country she would not have chosen for him, the country she would not have imagined that God would have chosen. Very frequently women are called upon to move to other cities, even other countries for the sake of their families. How can we use Mary as a model in these situations?*

3. *We know Mary had deep faith and absolute trust in God. Did this mean that she never felt fear or anxiety concerning her child?*

Mary at the Presentation
Luke 2:22-35

MARY and Joseph went up to the temple for the ceremony of the purification. This was, no doubt, before they left for Egypt. Jewish law declared a woman unclean after the birth of a child. For a son this was forty days.

Mary's forty days were now complete and so she and Joseph went to fulfil the law. They, being poor, were to offer two doves. Mary stayed in the Court of the Women while Joseph proceeded into what was called the Court of Israel where only men could enter. There a priest took Joseph's gift up to the altar and performed the rite.

The ceremony was not a long one. It marked, however, an official event in the life of the family. And, for devout Jews like Mary and Joseph, it was always a delight to go to the temple and to take part in any kind of worship.

They did not merely leave their offering and immediately return home. We can imagine them showing the temple to the baby Jesus, the way any parent would, even though they knew that he was much too young to understand it all.

While they were in the temple, they met a man named Simeon. He was a good and God-fearing man, who had spent many years serving God and praying for the salvation of Israel. God had responded to his prayers, telling Simeon that he would not die before having seen the Messiah. How and when the Messiah would come, he did not know. But he knew he would.

Now on this day Simeon was led into the temple by the Holy Spirit. This was to be the day he would see the Messiah. Surely when he arrived that day, he did not know quite what to expect. He may have expected to see a grown man. But as soon as he saw the baby with Mary and Joseph, he knew that this was he.

He went over to them. "May I hold the baby?" he may have asked. There was something in his manner, his bearing, and his obvious holiness that made Mary and Joseph trust him. They allowed him to hold the baby.

As Simeon held the child, his face must have glowed. He was holding the one he had yearned for so long. Then he was praying in an audible voice. Mary and Joseph heard him thank God for this privilege of now having seen the Savior. Now he was ready to die. God had kept his promise to him.

Mary and Joseph were amazed at what he was saying.

All along they believed God's message, but each time the meanings became stronger and stronger. Here Jesus was called not only the one to give glory to Israel, but also a light to Gentiles.

Mary had little time to ponder this just then, for Simeon was now blessing her and Joseph. Then he gave the baby back to her and spoke directly to her:

> *"You see this child: he is destined for the fall and for the rising of many in Israel, destined to be a sign that is rejected — and a sword will pierce your own soul too — so that the secret thoughts of many may be laid bare."*

Simeon left them shortly afterwards, no doubt feeling that now his life was complete.

Mary wanted only to hold the child closer to her, and to contemplate what the holy old man had said.

He was destined for the rise and fall of many. This child would make all the difference in the lives of many. He would be a sign that would be rejected. Already it was becoming clear that Jesus would not be accepted by all, perhaps not by most. And she herself would have a sword pierce her heart. If it had not been clear before, it was certainly clear now. The life of her son and her own life would be lives of suffering.

Mary would gladly have saved her son from suffering. But she knew very well that this could never be. Suffering was part of what his coming would be all about. Her gift was to be able to share it with him.

We can look at Mary holding her marvelous child in her arms, and we can dimly understand what she must have been feeling that day. No woman ever knows what her son or daughter will be called on to do in his or her life. There is likely to be much suffering. In fact, the greater things the child is called on to do in life, the more likely that suffering will be an accompaniment. And any time a child suffers, the mother suffers too.

Mary did not know just when or how things would happen. None of us are given to know these things. And no doubt it is just as well. We could not bear things if we had to anticipate them. The day the sufferings arrive is soon enough. And that is the time God gives the grace to bear it.

DISCUSSION:

1. *There are few loves stronger than that of a mother for a child. Because of this strong love, there is likely to be suffering for the mother when the child is suffering. What can we learn from Mary about enduring suffering because of children?*

2. *Mary knew Jesus' specialness, yet, as this story tells us, she was at times amazed at the responses his very presence called for in people. What does this tell us about Mary's faith and knowledge at this time?*

3. *We know that Simeon's prophecy came true in a most startling way when Jesus died on the cross. For Mary, all this was hidden. What value is there in the fact that God keeps the future hidden from us?*

Anna in the Temple

Luke 2:36-38

THE day that Mary and Joseph took Jesus to the temple was a momentous one in his life and theirs. It must have been clear to Mary and Joseph on this day that, wherever their son went, he would affect other people's lives. And he was still only forty days old.

This day in the temple, after the offering had been made, they had met the old man Simeon who had prophesied concerning Jesus and Mary. Now, while they were still contemplating the meaning of what Simeon had said, they met an old woman, the prophetess Anna.

Anna, we are told, had been married seven years, and then had been widowed; she was now eighty-four years old. She spent all her time in the temple, worshipping God, fasting and praying.

She was probably well-known to temple worshippers. When strangers came to the temple, they may have seen her and asked others about her. "Oh," we can imagine the response, "she is here all the time. She is the daughter of Phanuel, of the tribe of Asher."

When she spoke, people listened. She was an authentic prophetess. Her life was evidence of her closeness to God.

Now she came up to Mary and Joseph and the baby Jesus. We can imagine her stopping them and looking at the baby. At her advanced age, she was probably small and bent. But she commanded respect.

Because she was known to be a prophetess, it is likely that wherever she went in the temple, people were around. They wanted to hear what she might say. In this situation, after looking at the child, she must have turned her attention back to Mary and Joseph. We can see her with her clear eyes looking straight at them. Then she turned to the people around her, thanked God and spoke about the child to all who were waiting for God to redeem Israel. Did she tell them that this child would be the Redeemer? Or was her message veiled? We simply do not know. It must have been clear to Mary and Joseph, however, that this woman had recognized Jesus for who he was.

Anna is one of the holy women of the Bible. She was one of those ascetic and devout Jews who longed for the Messiah. In some ways she is like John the Baptist. She knew the savior would come, and she would prepared herself for him the best she could, just as John did. Her method of preparation was to live a life devoted completely to God. John the Baptist went out into the desert. Anna came to the temple and simply never left.

One wonders how she managed this. The Scriptures tell us that day and night she worshipped God. Of course, she must have slept sometime and she could not completely fast. But it does seem that she put aside all earthly needs as much as possible.

In today's busy world, a life of austerity seems very foreign. Yet there has been a long tradition in the Church, sanctified by Jesus himself with his fast in the desert, of the value of putting aside earthly needs for a while. If it is done rightly and with the right intention, fasting can be a very freeing experience. In the case of Anna, it brought her close to God, and gave her a sensitivity to God's presence about her. She is to be admired, not for her austerity in itself, but for the way it brought her to God.

It is also interesting to note that she is called a prophetess. A prophet or prophetess, of course, was not a fortuneteller, but someone especially called by God to be his messenger. Anna was not the first woman in Jewish history to be called a prophetess. The Jews understood that God was free to choose whomever he would to be his messenger, male or female.

Anna is also a model of older women. Many older women today, after their children are grown, are now able to take a more active part in the life of the Church. They go to daily Mass, take part in Bible discussions, and are always there to provide the service the Church needs. In some parishes these women are taken for granted or more or less discounted.

But people who discount them are mistaken. Many of these older women are like the prophetess Anna. They are close to God, and they need to be listened to.

DISCUSSION:

1. *Compare the story of Simeon and that of Anna in the Scriptures. Much more is told us of Simeon's message. Why do you think this is?*

2. *The aged prophetess Anna seems to be genuinely respected in the temple. How are older women treated in parishes that you are familiar with?*

3. *Notice that the Scriptures tell us that Anna spent her time worshipping God. How can one today devote a life to God's worship?*

Mary When Jesus Stayed in the Temple
Luke 2:41-52

THIS story gives us one of the most human pictures of Mary that we have. She is acting the way you or I may have acted.

The family went to Jerusalem every year for the Passover. This was a religious holiday, one that combined the expression of the deeply-felt faith of this family with the pleasure of a holiday and family gathering. Families shared and traveled together. Among the Jews, families tended to live in the same town near each other. They all knew each other very well. We can imagine Mary, Joseph, and Jesus joining with their relatives. We have surrounded the Holy Family with haloes; we put the emphasis on holy. Their relatives and friends put the emphasis on family. They were family above all else, doing what all families of Israel did.

For one thing, they didn't treat Jesus like a baby. When a Jewish boy was twelve years old, he had finished his basic schooling and was ready to be admitted into adult Jewish life. Certainly Mary and Joseph didn't take him by the hand and lead him into the temple. On the journey, he was no doubt in the group all the time but among his friends.

It was a true joy for him and his friends to go up to Jerusalem. Jerusalem and the temple were the greatest delights for Jewish people. For them the temple was truly the house of God. Devout Jews looked upon the temple and felt a thrill of happiness: they were God's chosen people and he was dwelling among them.

So with all this in mind, Mary and Joseph spent a happy religious holiday at the temple and in Jerusalem. And then they started home. Again they traveled with their friends, mostly walking. Mary probably traveled with the women and Joseph with the men. By nightfall, however, when they made their first camp, the families started rounding up their children. But Jesus was not to be found.

We can imagine the panic that Mary and Joseph must have felt. Where was he? He must have stayed in Jerusalem; there was nothing to do but to go back there and look for him.

It is likely they waited until dawn to go back. Travel at night would have been difficult with no lights, unless the moon was full and it was cloudless. It is hard to imagine them sleeping. Mary was a woman like the rest of us, and we have no trouble imagining all sorts of terrible things happening to our son.

Then it took them another full day to return to Jerusalem. Probably also some relatives went with them. We know from such stories as that of the Good Samaritan, that robbers made the roads unsafe for the single traveler.

They would have arrived the next night in Jerusalem. It would have been late and not the time to go to the temple. Perhaps they spent the night outside the city, since we know that even in the best of times Jerusalem was crowded. We can imagine Mary looking over the city that night and wondering just where Jesus was.

At first light they made their way into the city. Where to look? On the previous trip, besides going to the temple, the holy family and their traveling companions would probably have visited the bazaar. Was it possible that Jesus had remained with a friendly shopkeeper?

They found Jesus eventually, talking to the Jewish teachers, listening to them and asking them questions. We can imagine Mary and Joseph walking in and seeing him there. Perhaps the priests and Jesus were so engrossed that at first they didn't notice them.

We can appreciate how Mary would have felt. She was very happy and much relieved to see Jesus. But she did what you or I might do. She did not immediately say how happy she was to see him. She expressed to him the anguish and sorrow she had been feeling. Why did you do this? We have just spent a painful three days. Remember that in the Jewish way of reckoning, this would be the third day, just as Christ rose from the dead on the third day.

Jesus answered that of course, he would be in his Father's house. But he did go home with them, leaving behind some wondering people. The priests who had talked to him had been astonished. We have no record of what he said, but perhaps he was already questioning them about the conflict between the letter of the law and the spirit. Mary wondered too. Sometimes we imagine that she went around thinking all the time, My son is the Son of God. But apparently it was not like that.

Similarly, we don't quite understand each other or our children. The love of a mother is one of the strongest forces in the world. But love is more like acceptance than understanding. Certainly this incident in the temple was not the only time that Jesus did something that Mary did not understand. But she accepted it.

What a beautiful picture this is not only of a family relationship, but of any human relationship. We frequently do not understand each other. Love and acceptance in many cases are all we can handle. But perhaps they are enough. Understanding will come later.

DISCUSSION:

1. *Does this story give you a more human picture of Mary?*
2. *What kind of message was Jesus giving Mary and Joseph by staying behind in the temple?*
3. *Is it possible to truly understand another person?*

Mary at Cana
John 2:1-10

PICTURE this scene: a joyous, even boisterous wedding celebration, with Mary and Jesus in the crowd. Mary and Jesus were invited and then, it seems, because of Jesus, his disciples were invited. Weddings in those days in Israel were big, joyous affairs. Whenever Jesus wants to speak of a celebration, he uses the example of a wedding feast.

There was much eating and drinking — apparently more than was expected. The host ran out of wine. Here Mary, who may well have been a relative, noticed what was happening. We can imagine the embarrassment of the wedding family. Mary decided to do something about it.

Now, up to this time, Jesus had not worked any miracles. But Mary knew that she could count on Jesus to help. She turned to him and said simply, "They are out of wine." It is worth noting that this first miracle was not worked to cure anyone, nor was it one which solved any great world crisis. It was worked simply to save some poor people from an embarrassing situation. Further, the first miracle was done to produce some more wine which had no other purpose than to make the party merrier. Certainly it was not because the group was thirsty!

Thus, if we look at this scene we see one of the few times where Jesus and Mary are just plain having a good time. Certainly they must have celebrated many other occasions together. But here we have for all the world an example.

Jesus apparently wants to be with us in our recreation as well as in our work.

Although Jesus responded rather negatively when Mary told him about the wine running out, she knew him well. He would not refuse her. She told the servants, "Do whatever he tells you."

And so Jesus told the servants to fill up the water jars. Some Scripture scholars have expressed astonishment at what a large quantity of wine that was — six stone jars each capable of holding between twenty and thirty gallons. A conservative estimate is thus 120 gallons of wine!

What is also impressive is that this is quality wine. Jesus never does anything for people in a half-hearted way. If he works a miracle, it is to produce the best and the most.

And he did it at the request of Mary.

Mary here is very womanlike. She is a sensitive woman; she has served often enough to know the needs of others. And she cares. She wants to help these people have a nice party. So she turns to Jesus. She does not tell him what to do. Jesus is now grown up. He is no longer her little boy. But he cannot refuse her anything. It is as if he had plans to start his ministry a little later, but now, since Mary asked him, he will start right now. So he works a loving miracle.

The Gospel lesson shows a very loving Jesus, a loving and caring Mary, and a beautiful relationship between the two. It also shows us a good time. Sometimes we imagine that Mary and Jesus were always serious. But can we not imagine that Mary and Jesus would be fun people to have at a party? They would make others feel good, they would be happy they came, they would laugh and enjoy being with their friends.

DISCUSSION:

1. *What do you think of the fact that the first public miracle Jesus worked was one of producing more wine for a wedding party?*

2. *How do you see the interaction between Mary and Jesus in this story? His first answer seems harsh, but Mary knows him better than that.*

3. *Have you been burdened with the image that Mary and Jesus were always serious, that somehow fun and religion don't mix?*

Peter's Mother-in-Law

Mark 1:29-30

HERE we meet a mother-in-law. We also learn in this short passage that Peter was married.

Jesus had come to Capernaum, the town where he worked many miracles. It, not Nazareth, was called his own town. Here he was almost always well received.

The day of this miracle he went first to the synagogue and taught there. The people were astonished at the authority of his teaching. He also ordered an evil spirit out of a man.

He had had a busy morning. Now it was time for some lunch and relaxation. We can imagine Peter inviting him to his home. Peter and his brother would have been proud to have the Gentle Master come to their house.

When they arrived there, however, there was a problem. Peter's mother-in-law was sick in bed with a high fever.

It doesn't seem that Peter knew about this illness and invited Jesus there just to cure her. Rather, Jesus was told of her illness as soon as he got there.

Jesus went to the sick room. He looked at her, then he took her hand and helped her get up. Immediately, we are told, the fever left her. She felt much better. Her cure was instant.

Anyone who has been in bed even a short time knows how weak one feels afterwards. In this case, however, her cure was so instant and so complete, that she felt her normal self again. She got up and began to serve Jesus, Peter, and the rest.

Wherever Jesus went, crowds gathered around. Here the news of his cure spread rapidly, and before this day was over, many of the other sick people of Capernaum came and asked to be cured. Some of them came just to see Peter's mother-in-law, now restored to health. And Jesus cured all who asked.

We can imagine this woman. Peter, although it is mentioned elsewhere that he was older than John, was probably not much older. Perhaps he was in his twenties. His mother-in-law was probably only about forty. Following the Jewish custom of families living close together, she may have been living in with her daughter. Or perhaps that was a temporary arrangement while Peter was away on his travels with Jesus. Whether she lived here full-time or not, she was clearly not here as a guest. It was she who set about serving Jesus and the others. Her daughter, the wife of Peter, is not mentioned at all. Nor do we know much of his brother Andrew's situation. The home is said to be that of Simon and Andrew. Yet the person to be found here is Simon's mother-in-law.

There have been so many snide remarks about mothers-in-law. They are supposedly the ones who make life miserable for their sons- and daughters-in-law. They are the ones who never quite accept their child's spouse — who could ever be good enough for that precious child? Always they are the butt of jokes.

Yet, as many people will attest, the mother-in-law is as fine a woman as the mother. As always, the jokes are based on a few cases. Yet, the title of mother-in-law in our society is not one which is respected.

Peter must not have had mother-in-law problems. He was concerned with her, and because he told Jesus about her, she was cured. As soon as she was cured, she set to work helping others.

This is more likely the image of the real mother-in-law. She serves. The typical woman is always serving. For her own family she serves. She it is who sees to it that others have what they need. When her sons and daughters grow up and marry, she is still concerned with serving. Peter's mother-in-law had to serve many people. At sundown the whole town came to their house.

There is something else we must never forget about a mother-in-law. When we have a loving husband or wife, we need to remember who taught him or her how to be loving. It was assuredly his or her mother. When we have a kind spouse, one who devotes himself or herself to us, we need to remember where he or she learned that example. In fact, we need to remember to thank the mother-in-law for preparing for us and giving us the person in our lives we love the most. Service is her name.

Mothers, grandmothers, mothers-in-law all work together to provide for the children. Ultimately, men may do amazing things on a world level. But it is the women at home who see to it that the daily lives of children are still safe and secure.

DISCUSSION:

1. *What do you think of mother-in-law jokes? Where do you think such jokes originated?*

2. *It is significant in this story that the cure of Peter's mother-in-law was instant. Do you think it is also significant that she immediately began to serve those who were there?*

3. *How do you picture the wife of Peter?*

Jesus Raises the Widow's Son

Luke 7:11-17

THE little town called Nain has one claim to fame: it was where Jesus brought to life the widow's son. Jesus had come to this town on his travels around the country preaching, teaching, curing, and helping. As he was about to enter the gate of the village, he had to step back. A funeral procession was coming out. Someone was soon to be buried in the cemetery which was outside the walls of the town. We can imagine Jesus and the large crowd with him standing there watching this sad procession. Soon the whispers went around: "Look at her, the mother. She is a widow. This was her only son. How unhappy she must be."

It is quite possible that she was so overwhelmed in her grief that she did not even see the crowd. When sorrow is that great there is no room for anything else. She had reason to be sorrowful. A widow in Israel in those days was truly to be pitied. Women, considered to be weaker, were to be protected by men. The young girl was under her father's protection. When she married, that protection was transferred to her husband. If he died, she could expect her sons to look after her. But this woman had lost all.

Especially she had lost her only son. Even today, families want a son to carry on the family name, the whole family heritage, the bloodline. For this woman it was all over.

She moved forward, behind the procession, weighed down with her sorrow. Everyone felt pity for her. But there was one in the crowd whose pity prompted him to do something.

It is interesting that this woman did not ask Jesus to raise her son; she did not ask anything. She was too bowed in her grief to do that. She said nothing in this whole story. We do not even know her name. But it was Jesus who reached out to her. He went over to her and said, "Don't cry."

We can imagine her reaction. This stranger came over to her and told her to stop weeping at the time in her life when weeping is most appropriate. She must have looked at him, puzzled. Perhaps she had heard of Jesus, heard of his miracles. But she had never thought of asking him for one. She might have just stared at him.

He stopped the procession. He went over to the men who were carrying out the dead man on a bier. They stopped and waited. Everyone waited. He touched the bier. Then he, who could command the forces of nature, spoke another command: "Young man! Get up, I tell you."

Immediately the young man got up, and he started to talk. One wonders what he said. The people all stood around in amazement.

Jesus again took command. We read that Jesus gave him to his mother. We can picture this. Jesus took the young man by the hand, and led him to his mother, who was watching with a mixture of awe, astonishment, and sheer happiness. Her son was alive!

And that is all we know about this story. But what a beautiful story it is. Jesus worked a very great miracle here without being asked, impromptu, so to speak, simply because he felt pity for this woman. What a message this gives us about the kind of person Jesus is. He cares! He feels compassion and pity. And never did he feel that this widow, certainly no important person even in her little town of Nain, was unimportant. Her sorrow touched him.

Jesus has not changed. Today he still understands our sorrows, even before we tell him about them. He will not think our sorrows are foolish or that what we suffer about is unimportant. Sometimes we forget, in our desire to be strong people, that natural sorrows are not to be despised. Nor should we close our hearts to the natural compassion we may feel at the sufferings of others. Rather, like Jesus, we should look to what we can do to relieve such sufferings. This story brings us close to the heart of the Christian message — that our God loves and cares about us, and that we are most like him when we do the same for others.

DISCUSSION:

1. *When you contemplate this story, can you imagine yourself in the place of this widow? What would be your feelings when your son is brought to life again?*

2. *Can you think of other instances in the Scriptures where Jesus is shown as having compassion? What kinds of people or occasions seem to bring this on?*

3. *Can you think of examples in your own life or others' lives, when just as it seemed all hope was gone, some marvelous intervention occurred?*

The Woman at Simon's House
Luke 7:36-50

JESUS was at dinner. He had been invited and he went. Have you noticed in the Bible how frequently Jesus went out to dinner with friends? In this case his host was Simon, a Pharisee.

He was at table, not seated there, but lying on a couch, head toward the table, feet away from it. Diners reclined on their left arms and used their right hands for eating.

There Jesus was, eating and easily seen from the street. Houses in Israel in those days were fairly open. The climate was hot a good part of the year, and of course there was no air-conditioning. So it was natural to have as open an arrangement as possible.

A certain woman came by. She had heard that Jesus would be there today. As soon as she had found out where he was, she hurried to see him, bringing from her home one of her most valuable possessions. She was carrying it now, the heavy jar bulky under her arm.

She looked into the house and saw Jesus; she had wanted to see him for a long time. Maybe she would have preferred to see him alone, talk to him privately. She was fully aware of her sinfulness and she knew that the people most likely to reject her were the Pharisees, one of whom was Simon. But she knew Jesus would not reject her.

Most likely she had heard him speak at one time or another. We can picture her hanging at the edge of a crowd listening to him, finding his words reaching her heart. But her reputation was well-known in the town. Others drew away from her as she moved by. People in the crowd pulled their cloaks closer around them to avoid any physical contact.

But she knew that Jesus would not reject her. And now she knew what she would do. She moved right in and went straight to Jesus. She did not say a word. She stood at his feet and the closeness of the contact overwhelmed her.

She began to weep as she had never wept before in her life. She could not control herself. Her tears covered Jesus' feet. With each tear, though, she felt that some of the weight of the past was falling from her.

Jesus' feet were all wet. She had no towel. All she had was her long luxurious hair which she now pulled forward and used to wipe his feet. Then she poured the expensive perfume all over his feet, so thickly and so extravagantly that the whole house was filled with the aroma.

Everyone was watching her. She did not look at anyone but Jesus, but the others were watching and criticizing. Simon, Jesus' host, was criticizing Jesus too. Surely, he thought to himself, if Jesus were really a prophet he would know this woman was a sinner and would not allow her to touch him.

And Jesus knew it all. He knew the woman's sins, but he also knew the love and sorrow in her heart. And he knew the criticism in Simon's heart. He praised the woman for her faith and her love, that faith and love which exceeded those of Simon.

Then Jesus told her, "Your sins are forgiven."

Others were astonished, but the woman was not. She knew Jesus would forgive her sins. She left that house that day a different woman. She had given extravagantly of herself and she had been forgiven. Her whole life was changed.

What a beautiful story this is. How much it shows of Jesus' way of looking at things. Have you ever noticed that Jesus rarely criticized sinners? He was always patient and loving with them, eager to forgive. The only times we find him condemning is with those who found fault with others or set themselves above others.

Jesus is not the one who criticizes. He forgives.

He recognizes the need to be extravagant sometimes, to break the jar of perfume and pour out the whole thing. Not to give just a little and save the bottle for future times, but to give all.

This story has a special message for women. The woman in this story acted in a truly feminine way. When we women love we always want to show our love, not just say it. We do not philosophize about love. We give it simply and fully, as this woman did. Her manner of giving was so feminine — the tears over Jesus' feet, the wiping with her hair, the perfume. And Jesus accepted it all. Never once does he laugh at a woman like this one. Nor does he permit others to laugh or criticize. He simply loves and forgives. Through the ages, women have not hesitated to go to Jesus and his response has always been the same.

All the rational arguments of the world break down over a simple act of love.

DISCUSSION:

1. *What are the characteristics of Jesus that this story shows?*

2. *What do you feel as you read this story and compare it to the way that many, maybe sometimes ourselves, treat a woman of this type?*

3. *Are you ever like those who complain that what this woman did was too extravagant, too theatrical?*

The Samaritan Woman

John 4:1-42

SAMARITANS were considered something worse than foreigners. They were considered heretics, outcasts, excommunicated. Bitter hatred existed between them and the Jews.

This woman was doubly an outcast — she was not only a member of this hated group, but she was a notorious sinner. She had apparently been married and divorced five times. She was now living with man number six, whom, it seems, she had not married. Men in those days could easily repudiate a wife; it was not so easy for women. But five times was excessive for anyone.

It is interesting that this woman came to the well alone at the middle of the day. Most of the women would have come in the early morning; it would have been part of their morning chores to get the water for the day. Then they would see their friends and chat about their families and the little things that happened in the village. This woman did not come in the morning. No doubt she knew very well that they looked down on her for her style of life. She came alone, at mid-day. She was the kind of woman who was independent enough to come by herself. And, it is likely she told herself, she didn't need the other women.

She was very surprised when Jesus spoke to her, as were the disciples later on when they returned. Jews did not talk to Samaritans, nor did men and women talk to each other in public.

And what did Jesus say? He started by asking a favor: "Give me a drink of water." How interesting this is, considering that Jews and Samaritans would never even drink from the same cup. Jesus did not do anything for her at first; he asked her to do something for him.

It was his way of getting a conversation started with her. Soon he told her that if she knew who he was, she would ask for water from him. She went along with it. She found him intriguing and then even a little too much.

"Call your husband," he said.

"Sir, I have no husband."

Right, Jesus said, "you have had five and the one you now have is not your husband."

Notice how quickly then she changed the subject. She did not want to talk about her messed-up life. This is a woman who has been condemned by her own people and who has learned to shrug it aside. But she is not impervious. In fact, one gets the idea that if she had been more accepted by her people, she might not be living as she did. Notice that she does not appear in this story repentant, as Mary Magdalene was. When she went to the well that day, she had no idea what would happen. But her meeting with Jesus changed her life. It changed the lives of the townspeople too. Later, when all the people believed in Jesus, they even told her that they accepted him on his own, not because of her word. So perhaps they didn't really even accept her then. But, by then, she had changed.

We never hear another word about her. But we can well imagine that her life was different after the day at the well.

We never know what will happen to us either. We may meet Christ in the person of someone we least expect, and that person will change our lives.

Jesus never mixed up things that were merely cultural with things that mattered in eternity. In this case he brushed aside the whole idea of men and women not talking to each other in public. He wanted to talk to this woman. She needed him.

He also never allowed prejudices to stand in the way of human need. This woman needed him, Samaritan or not.

We have a way of making certain people outcasts. By doing this we deprive those persons of community support, but we thus deprive ourselves of the gifts that these persons have to offer. Each person we meet, it seems, gives us a gift. One teaches us one aspect of life, another person may teach us some other vital truth. Here the Samaritan woman, the outcast, was able to give the gift of the Messiah to her whole community.

DISCUSSION:

1. *What does this story teach us about the way Jesus perceives us, as opposed to the way we sometimes perceive each other?*

2. *Is the world of today very much different from the world that separated Jews from Samaritans? What would be modern examples of this same process in operation and its effects?*

3. *What can we learn from the fact that Jesus selected this woman to reveal that he was the Messiah?*

The Woman Who Touched Jesus' Cloak

Mark 5:25-34

THIS woman was truly to be pitied. We know that among the Jewish people in those days, as among many other peoples, bleeding rendered a person legally unclean. This, of course, affected women regularly. For seven days after each menstrual flow, forty days after the birth of a son, and eighty days after the birth of a daughter, women could not take part in temple worship or even take full part in family ceremonies. Their uncleanness was contagious. An unclean woman could render others unclean if she touched them.

Here we have a woman who had a type of bleeding that had lasted for twelve years. She had done all she could for a cure, going from doctor to doctor, spending all her money on them, but to no avail. Instead of getting better, she got worse. How unhappy she must have been, not being able to be a true part of the worshipping community for twelve years. How desperate she was for a cure.

She was afraid to approach Jesus. According to Jewish law, he would be rendered unclean if he touched her. But, oh, she wanted so much to be cured. She knew he could cure others, but her disease was of a different kind. She did not know how she could ask him to cure her.

She had a plan. Perhaps she could touch just his garment as he went by. His power was real. She had seen that. Maybe a little of that power would flow out to her.

She stationed herself in such a way that she would be near him as he went by. And then, as he was being crowded in on all sides, and as his attention was drawn away to the man Jairus pleading for Jesus to cure his daughter, she reached out and gently, but with deep faith, touched his cloak. She said to herself, "If I but touch his garment, I shall be cured."

As the bleeding stopped immediately, the joy began to rise in her. She would have been content to slip away quietly savoring her cure, but that was not to be.

Jesus stopped, turned away from Jairus, and asked, "Who touched me?"

His disciples were surprised at the question. With the crowds pushing around, it would have been strange, they said, if he had not been touched. It couldn't be helped. No, Jesus insisted, someone had touched him in a special way. He had felt power going out from him.

Now the woman knew she had to come forward. She was afraid. A moment before she had felt full of joy, but now she was full of fear. She knew that she had violated the law by touching Jesus. Had she rendered the Great Teacher unclean?

She came forward slowly, as people cleared a space around her. She fell at Jesus' feet. Then she raised her eyes and looked at him. She did not see anger in his eyes, only compassion. That look gave her courage and, in a trembling voice, she told the whole story of why and how she had touched his cloak. Some of the people standing around listening were indignant. But not Jesus.

He looked straight at her and with a clear voice said, "My daughter, your faith has saved you. Go in peace and be free from your trouble."

She must have barely known how to thank him. As the crowd moved on and she remained, what peace must have filled her. She must have felt lighter than air. After twelve long and very disturbing years, she was now cured.

What a beautiful picture we have here of a loving and very understanding Jesus. He was helping a woman who was in a most embarrassing situation. He knew that she was cured and he could have chosen to simply ignore it. That is what at the time she would have preferred. But he chose to call attention to her cure for our sake. We needed to know that he can cure us of even embarrassing situations. Even more important, he rose above the local prejudices. The needs of this woman were greater than concern about any taboo.

And so was her faith. Jesus attributed her cure to her faith. He did this frequently as he cured people on his travels through Israel. Without faith on the part of people, he said, he could not perform any cures. He can and wants to do anything for us. We need only to ask with faith.

DISCUSSION:

1. *This is a very womanly story. We can easily understand this woman's approach in the light of the customs of the people. What does this story tell us about Jesus' attitude toward any custom that was harmful or restrictive to the needs of people?*

2. *Does Jesus still cure people today? How important is faith when we approach Jesus with our requests for cures (physical or otherwise)?*

3. *Why did Jesus make a public issue of this incident? What do you imagine the people standing by during this incident said or did?*

The Daughter of Jairus
Mark 5:35-43

JAIRUS was an official at the local synagogue. He had no doubt heard Jesus preach many times. He had witnessed miracles. Perhaps up to this time he was somewhat skeptical. As long as he was not personally in need of a cure or miracle, he could afford the luxury of skepticism.

But then his daughter fell ill. This was his darling little daughter, the joy of his life. Now he sought out Jesus. If before he had been indifferent or skeptical, now he was willing to acknowledge Jesus totally. He fell at Jesus' feet and made an act of faith.

"My little daughter is very sick. Please come and lay your hands on her and she will get well and live."

Jesus agreed to go with him. How eager Jairus must have been for Jesus to hurry. He may have made every effort to get the crowds to let Jesus through. This was not easy. Jesus was being crowded on every side.

In the midst of all that crowd a woman who suffered from a hemorrhage came up and touched his cloak. Jesus cured her but he took a moment to let her know that what she did was all right. We can imagine that Jairus would have been as excited as everyone else during the cure, but eager for Jesus to hurry on. His daughter was dying, Jesus had to come right away.

And then his worst fears were realized. Some men were coming from his neighborhood. He could tell by the way they were approaching him that they had bad news.

"Jairus," they told him sadly, "your daughter is dead." They added that he need not bother the Teacher any more, he might as well come home and take care of funeral arrangements.

Jairus, standing next to Jesus, must have been crushed. My daughter, he thought, my darling daughter. If only Jesus had gotten there in time.

Jesus said to him, "Pay no attention to them. Only believe." With all his heart, Jairus must have made a deep act of faith.

By now they were near Jairus' house. Jesus stopped and told the crowds to wait. He took with him only his three closest disciples, Peter, James, and John, and along with Jairus they went to the house.

When they arrived there, the funeral weeping and mourning was already going on. It was customary to have paid mourners who chanted lamentations, as well as flute players. Between these two there was likely to be a frenzy of noise at a funeral.

"Why all this confusion and noise?" Jesus asked. "The girl is not dead, only asleep." The mourners laughed. They had seen her and they knew she was dead.

But Jesus put them out of the house. Then he took with him Jairus and his wife and together they entered the room where the little girl lay on the bed. Jesus took her by the hand and said to her, "Little girl, get up." As her parents watched, the little girl got up immediately. She started to walk around.

Her parents stared at her in awe. Jairus had expected Jesus to cure his little girl. Jesus had told him to believe and he believed. And yet he was still so amazed that he could only stare. It was one thing to cure the sick; even doctors with their skills sometimes did that. But to bring someone back from the dead was a totally different thing. That was reserved to God alone.

It took Jesus to bring him and the little girl's mother back to earth. "Give her something to eat," he said.

At this, the girl's mother must have taken her to the kitchen and given her some food. The mother and father must have watched with amazement and joy as their daughter displayed a young and healthy appetite.

Jesus left them then, warning them not to tell anyone. But, of course, they didn't need to tell anyone. The news traveled easily enough.

We hear nothing more about Jairus and his wife and their twelve-year-old daughter. But we do know how much Jairus must have loved and valued his daughter. In spite of the fact that women in many countries were not valued and daughters were less esteemed than sons, we all know how a lovely daughter can captivate any man's heart. On an intellectual level perhaps sons were more valued; on a personal and emotional level, people loved their daughters as much, or even more.

Nor did Jesus think that it was a waste of his power, so to speak, to bring to life a young girl. And here, he displayed a great deal of sensitivity: reassuring the father, putting the mourners out of the house, taking only the parents into the room with him, and finally his telling them to give the girl something to eat.

Jairus' daughter had been brought to life by God's Son. She was special. But then she only proved what we know of Jesus: no one, male or female, young or old, is insignificant in his eyes. Each person is worth his attention.

DISCUSSION:

1. *Jesus raised three persons to life in the Scriptures: Jairus' daughter, the son of the widow of Nain, and Lazarus. Why do you thing he chose this little girl along with the other two?*

2. *How do you picture the mother of this girl throughout this story? She may have been the one who sent her husband to Jesus, and she was the one who was with her when she died.*

3. *Does this story give us any insight into Jesus' attitude toward young people?*

Herodias

Mark 6:16-29

HERODIAS lived in luxury with her second husband, Herod. She had been married to Philip, Herod's brother. When Philip divorced her, Herod married her.

Herod was very interested in anything or anybody who was different. John the Baptist, to him, was a very interesting person.

What a contrast between John the Baptist and Herod. John looked rough and weathered. We know he spent years living in the desert, eating little, and praying. When he left the desert, it was only because he had a mission. When he saw sin, he called it sin. He would not be quiet. Herod was a man who lived a life of luxury in his palace, surrounded by servants who catered to his every whim.

John the Baptist had told him, "It is not right to take your brother's wife."

Herod must have had a secret admiration for anyone who spoke so boldly to him. After all, he was most likely surrounded by flatterers.

Herod would not have arrested John, but his wife Herodias urged him. In fact, she wanted him killed.

Herod did not want to kill John. Not only did he secretly admire him, but he may have been afraid of him. Herod was a man of power and he recognized power when he saw it. John had a power he could not fathom.

He arrested John and kept him in prison. In this manner he was able to at least temporarily satisfy the bloodthirsty Herodias. Also it gave him the opportunity to talk to John when he chose to do so.

Now and then he would go down to the dungeon and talk to John. John would never fail to point out his sins. It was as if John could read his life like an open book. This fascinated and frightened Herod. He would leave John's presence each time greatly disturbed. But he always came back.

His wife Herodias was frightened of John too. She knew what he said was true. But she did not want him saying it. She wanted him dead.

Then there was the night of Herod's birthday party. Everyone who was anyone was there. What a night they had, with drinking and loud talking and laughing all night.

It was getting late and Herod had already drunk a great deal. Now was Herodias' chance.

She helped her beautiful daughter Salome get dressed. She knew how Herod doted on this girl. Herodias could not always get her way with Herod, but this girl could.

Salome danced. She moved sensuously to the music. Every eye was on her. Even Herod, who had seen her dance before, was astonished. This girl was better than ever. As the crowd applauded, Herod called to her in a voice loud enough for everyone to hear.

"Salome," he said, "you have greatly pleased me. Now, what would you like to have? I promise you, with my solemn oath, that I will give you whatever you ask, even if you ask for half my kingdom!"

Salome smiled and bowed. She was not sure what she should ask for. Herodias must have smiled to herself. Ah, here was her chance. "Ask," she told her daughter, "for the head of John the Baptist."

Salome returned to Herod. She stood directly in front

of him at the table. All the others were around listening. What would this girl ask for?

"I want," she said, "the head of John the Baptist brought to me right now on a plate." And she picked up a plate from the table.

Herod, who had been half-drunk, was now instantly sober. Oh, no, he thought, anything but that. He looked around. Everyone was watching him. They had heard his promise. They had heard him swear. He could not go back on his word.

The girl was waiting and the whole crowd was listening. So he sent a guard to bring in the head of this holy man. And then suddenly he didn't feel like celebrating anymore.

The others may have sensed his change of mood. Perhaps people started to leave. By the time the head of John the Baptist was brought in, the party was over. Only the most blood-thirsty would have wanted to see that. Like Herodias. She must have rejoiced that her enemy was dead. And how was he her enemy? Only in that he pointed out her sins.

Herodias is not an admirable person. We can imagine her as a spoiled and sensuous woman, one who was accustomed to having her way and would even kill one who warned her.

She is a good example of a woman whose instincts have become perverted. There is a deadly strain in women. It is referred to in Rudyard Kipling's statement that "the female of the species is deadlier than the male." The reason is simply this. Women are physically weaker than men, but in no other way are they weaker. Women have been given great strength to do whatever is necessary to protect their children. Women are fighters for their children.

Now this strength can be perverted when it is used for

other means, as it was in this case. Herodias used her strength to have an innocent man killed. And only because he told her the truth.

DISCUSSION:

1. *Herodias is an example of a woman in the New Testament who does not seek forgiveness, or at least none is mentioned here. Is there anything we can learn from a story like hers?*

2. *Notice the way Herodias used people, her husband Herod and her daughter. What can be said of the way some people use others?*

3. *Herod was more frightened of John the Baptist than Herodias was. What do you make of that?*

The Woman Taken in Adultery

John 8:3-11

HERE we have a case of a woman who is a sinner. Never does she deny her guilt. Never does she pretend that what she has done is not wrong. She is caught in the very act of committing adultery.

Now the Jewish law considered adultery sinful for both men and women. Yahweh's commandment was absolute: "Thou shalt not commit adultery." But adultery was more harshly treated in a woman than in a man. A woman in marriage was seen as sort of the property of her husband.

Thus by committing adultery, she was perhaps giving her husband an heir that was not his. The interests of the family called for the most severe punishment for the woman. But adultery in a man did not do so much harm to the family, as the people at that time saw it. A man's adultery was a crime only if he seduced a married or a betrothed woman, because then he injured the family of another.

The law required that a woman actually caught in the act of adultery, be killed, here by stoning. So that is what the Scribes and Pharisees were planning to do. They didn't really care that much about this woman. This was rather a test case for Jesus. They knew that Jesus was claiming a higher law, one of love, and yet he stressed obedience to his Father. Now, they thought, they would trap him. If he said, she should be stoned, where would be his compassion that he was preaching? If he said she should not be stoned, they could accuse him of breaking the law.

For her part, the woman stood there. She did wrong by committing adultery and she knew it. No one, not her nor Jesus nor anyone else, ever denied her guilt. She stood there trembling while the men argued. They wanted to stone her to death.

The men who accused her hardly looked at her. They were ready to stone her whenever Jesus gave the word. She would have to die. There was no way out. But she didn't know Jesus.

He, at first, didn't seem to pay that much attention to her either. He bent down and started to write in the sand. We don't know what he wrote. Some say that he wrote the sins of the accusers. Others interpret the writing as a way of expressing disinterest. Clearly, by his every action, Jesus made it clear that he had no intention of judging and condemning this woman.

But these Scribes and Pharisees were not to be put off. They had every intention of forcing Jesus into a decision, one way or another. Finally, he looked up and said, "If there is one of you who has not sinned, let him be the first to throw a stone at her." Then he continued his writing.

The Scribes and Pharisees looked at each other. We know that some of these men were full of pride, but they were at least honest enough to admit that they were not without sin. They looked at their leader. He shook his head, put his stone down, and went away. He would not be the one to cast the first stone. The others dropped theirs too and went away.

Thus, within a short time, Jesus was alone with the woman. She did not run away. She could have, considering that Jesus certainly showed no inclination to harm her. But she stood there. We can imagine that she was waiting for him to say something. She waited.

Finally, he looked up and said, "Woman, where are they? Has no one condemned you?"

"No, sir," she replied.

"Well, then," Jesus said, "neither will I. Go and sin no more."

And with those few and simple words, she was forgiven, her slate wiped clean, and she was told simply to mend her ways.

And that is all there is to the story. We don't know what happened to this woman afterwards. Maybe she was tempted again, maybe her relationship with her husband was still an unhappy one. But that day when she walked away, she knew that she had found someone who could look into her heart and forgive her.

It is interesting that when the Bible mentions women who are sinners, it is usually sexual sin that they are accused of. Certainly this is not because that is the worst sin or the only one that women commit. It may simply be, in the Gospel stories, the one that was most obvious to outsiders — the woman of the streets or the woman taken in adultery. But Jesus easily forgave this sin. He was much more concerned with what was in the hearts of people.

What an encouraging story this is for women and others. The woman, the outcast, is forgiven and loved.

DISCUSSION:

1. *Is it possible that we reject Jesus' forgiveness because it is so easily and readily given?*

2. *Do we forgive ourselves as fast as we forgive others? We do not have a problem of God forgiving us. He does. We have a much harder time forgiving ourselves and each other.*

3. *Are we much quicker sometimes to criticize and condemn others than God would be? Why is this the case?*

Women Who Accompanied Jesus
Luke 8:1-3

FROM the very beginning, women as well as men followed Jesus. In this small passage, some of Jesus' closest women followers are mentioned. Mary Magdalene leads the list, as usual. Except for Mary, Jesus' mother, no other woman is ever so closely associated with Jesus as Mary

Magdalene. There is some confusion in the Gospels as to her identity. At times when a Mary is mentioned, it is not clear just who this is, but here the Mary is identified as the Magdalene, the one from whom Jesus had driven seven demons. The Scripture scholar John McKenzie says that these seven demons may well mean a disease rather than a life of sin. Yet we know that the Scriptures frequently consider sin to be the cause of illness. Thus, this Mary had a reputation of being a repentant sinner, someone whom Jesus had saved. In any case, she is always pictured as someone whose love for Jesus was extraordinary.

Another woman mentioned here is Joanna, identified as the wife of Chuza who was an officer in Herod's court. We know little of this Joanna except what is mentioned here. She is a contrast to Mary Magdalene, who was no doubt unmarried. Chuza was not necessarily in the military. He might have been a civilian officer engaged in some business connected with ruling the kingdom.

Joanna might have had to bear some of the brunt of the Jewish hatred of Herod's court. Also, she must have been something of an unusual woman. She was married, and yet she did not spend her time at home with her family. She followed Jesus and provided for his needs.

She reminds us of women today whose husbands provide well for them, but leave them at home alone a lot. Many of these women do what Joanna did; they devote their time to providing for the well-being of a religious leader. No doubt Joanna came in for her share of criticism.

Then there was Susanna. Nothing else is told of us but her name. Still she must have been significant in her time, or her name would not have been mentioned. In addition, the passage says, there were many other women. They helped the disciples with their belongings.

One can imagine this scene of roving people. They wandered the country as a group. Sometimes they stayed several days in a town, sometime they merely passed through. In each case, if the people were receptive, Jesus would preach for them. Maybe he would work miracles.

In some towns, Jesus and his disciples were invited to dine at the home of wealthy people, who alone, no doubt, had room for such a crowd. At other times the group must have camped on hillsides. Someone had to provide the food, someone had to take care of the clothes and all of the other services people need for even simple living.

The women mentioned here took care of many of the personal needs of Jesus and his disciples. As a reward, they were there whenever he preached. They were able to learn and absorb his message. And they must have found their faith and their love deepening every day.

They also would have shared in some of the criticism that the Pharisees and Scribes had for Jesus. Jesus was accused of eating and associating with sinners. Included in the sinners would have been some of Jesus' women followers. On one occasion, when Jesus ate at the house of Simon, Jesus' enemies criticized him for allowing a sinful woman to touch him when she washed his feet with her tears and wiped them with her hair.

Yet Jesus never told these women he did not want them with him. Instead they are praised for their steadfastness in following him. When he needed anything, they were there.

Women today still follow Jesus. Just as frequently, their work consists in providing for the material needs of the disciples. Certainly this is not the only service they may or should provide, but it is never one to be despised. With it comes the privilege of being there when Jesus speaks, as he certainly still does today.

DISCUSSION:

1. *Can you imagine the criticism that some of these women must have had to hear when they chose to follow Jesus around the country in order to provide for him? Does this kind of criticism still occur today?*

2. *What was the attitude of Jesus toward the women who followed him? Mention specific incidents if you can.*

3. *The role of women in the Church is much talked about today. Perhaps, though, there is no role, but roles. Whatever may be said, it is clear that from the beginning, women have played a part in the Church's ministry. What can you learn from this Scripture passage about women and ministry?*

Jesus' Relatives in Nazareth

Mark 6:1-6

HERE we have Jesus coming home to Nazareth. This was his home town, the place he was brought up. Here his family was well-known, here his mother still lived and his father Joseph had been the village carpenter.

On the Sabbath, Jesus began to teach in the synagogue. He did this frequently in other towns, especially in Capernaum. It was for him a golden opportunity to reach a large group of people.

At first, the people were amazed. How well he spoke, what beautiful words! Were did he learn all of this? Surely not in their own local little synagogue school when he was a boy.

Some people remembered him as the boy who played with their sons. Others recalled his teen-age years. Perhaps, as they looked back at him now, there was something different about him. But it is so hard for people who have seen someone grow up to realize how they have far outgrown their home town.

We can imagine Mary there in the synagogue too, listening to her son. How happy she must have been for him, how delighted to hear him preach. Then, after his speaking was over, she heard the comments and questions people were raising around her. "Where did he get all of this? How did he learn all this wisdom?"

Others were talking of his miracles. They had heard that he had performed many miracles in other cities, curing the sick, restoring sight to the blind, even raising the dead to life. How could he, a simple carpenter's son, do all of this?

Soon Mary realized that people were looking at her. She heard the whispers. We know this man, we know his family, his mother, his brothers and sisters (relatives). How could he do all of this? And then, why doesn't he do some of his miracles here in his home town?

Mary watched as Jesus responded to this murmuring. "Listen," he said, "no prophet is accepted in his home town."

A few sick people came to him and asked to be cured. He did heal a few of them. Most of them, he said, he could not cure because they did not have faith.

In a parallel passage in Luke 4:16-30, Jesus explained to his townspeople how other prophets were rejected in their home towns and even their own countries. He gave the example of Elijah who was sent to a widow of Zarephath in Sidon, out of Israelite territory, while there were many widows in Israel. Or Naaman the Syrian leper who was cured by Elisha, although there were many lepers in Israel.

Home town people simply cannot accept the prophets who have grown up among them.

The people of Nazareth were angry with him. They took him to the top of a hill and wanted to throw him down, but he passed through their midst and slipped away. His time for martyrdom had not yet come.

And so Jesus left Nazareth for good. He would never again return to speak in the synagogue. Mary and some other relatives of his would see him again, but not here. They would have to go around the country and seek him out.

We do not know about all the relatives of Jesus, but apparently some of them did not accept him. He specifically mentions that a prophet is accepted everywhere except in his home town, and by his relatives and his family.

We can imagine the problems this may have caused Jesus' family at home. Mary would have not been the kind of person to aggravate the situation, but everyone knew that she supported her son completely. Perhaps she lost friends because of Jesus. Certainly he would have been the cause of gossip for many days after this incident in Nazareth.

Mary herself, of course, was no ordinary woman. Yet, what was true for her son was true for her. Just as he was not recognized in his home town as anything special, neither was she. This is just Mary, people said, an ordinary woman, married to a carpenter.

At times it seems that any gain on a larger level is made at the expense of the loss of something at home. Many people even feel compelled to choose between their larger commitments and their home ones. Sometimes working women have such a cruel choice to make. If they wish to advance in their careers, it will be at the cost of something they would like to do for their families.

Even Mary had this choice to make. By fully accepting

her son and seeking him out wherever he might be around the country, she was rejecting the warm comfortable life she might have had at Nazareth. It seems clear from this passage that she had to break off from some of her relatives. But in a sense she had no choice. Jesus was her son and the Son of God. She had long since made her choice of him.

DISCUSSION:

1. *Does Nazareth seem very different from a modern small town in the way its citizens treated Jesus?*
2. *How do you think things were in Nazareth the day after this incident? How do you think people treated Mary?*
3. *Are conflicts between relatives fairly common? Why is this so? Are there ways relatives can overcome these problems?*

The Widow's Offering
Mark 12:41-44

JESUS sat near the temple treasury and watched as people contributed money. He saw many rich people giving large sums of money. Some of these people made quite a show about making contributions. They wanted others to know how generous they were.

Then came a poor little old woman, a widow. She did not want to make a scene of her giving. Perhaps she felt somewhat ashamed that she had so little to give. She put in two copper coins, worth about a penny. She put the money in and tried to slip away quietly.

But Jesus had seen her. He had been impressed enough that he called his disciples together. "Look at that widow," he said, "she gave more than all the rest." The disciples must have looked at him in wonder. More than the rest, they thought, why she gave only two small coins. "She gave more than the rest," Jesus went on, "because the others gave what they had left over. This woman gave of her substance, she gave from what she had to live on."

Widows were to be pitied in Israelite society. They had lost their husbands, their source of support. They may not have had children to look after them. Instead, they had to make do with what they had managed to save. Perhaps they and their husbands had made efforts to save money, but they may have had hard times. In any case, it was common then, as it is today, to find older widows living in rather poor circumstances.

Such was the case of this widow. Yet she felt the need to contribute to the temple treasury, seeing it as her gift to God. And her small gift did not go unnoticed.

Jesus was the type to notice such a gift. He had an unusual interest in the people that others ignored. The wealthy of the city, the high priests and Pharisees, no doubt considered widows of little interest. It was true that the Scriptures enjoined upon them to give to the widows and orphans, and no doubt they did occasionally; but as for treating them as persons worthy of respect, they had no time for that. The poor are rarely considered persons of equal value as the rich. Even as they are given help, they are frequently insulted.

But the value system of the world was not the value system of Jesus, nor should it be ours. Jesus knew what was in people's hearts. This woman gave more than all the rest,

Jesus said. And now, two thousand years later, we still have to learn this message.

Was this woman aware of Jesus talking about her and using her as an example to hold up to his disciples? Probably not. She gave her offering and disappeared. And yet all these years later, she is remembered.

We must never underestimate the weak and the poor of this world. Very frequently they accomplish more by their silent ministrations than the wealthy and powerful do with all their showy exhibitions. Jesus valued the poor. He never once treated them as second class. On the contrary, he seemed to have a preference for them. Unfortunately, today this lesson is still not learned. We have only to look around us to see that the poor are still considered somewhat lesser persons than the rich.

DISCUSSION:

1. *Why do you think Jesus sat where he could watch the contributions that people were making to the temple treasury?*

2. *Would some people tell this woman she was foolish to give at all to the temple treasury?*

3. *Do you agree that older people, especially older women, are not valued as much as young and strong persons are?*

The Crippled Woman
Luke 13:10-17

ON a quiet Sabbath, Jesus was teaching in a synagogue. He looked over the crowd who were listening to him and saw a mixed group. Some were his faithful disciples, hanging onto every word. Others were hearing him for the first time. Then there were some who had come only to criticize. Apparently both men and women were there, the men in the front seats, the women separated from the men in their own section.

As Jesus taught, he saw a woman bent over so badly that she could not sit up straight. But she stayed there, trying to listen. We do not know this woman's name. The Gospel simply tells us that she had an evil spirit in her for eighteen years that had caused this affliction.

We do not know if this was literally a case of possession. The persons of those times believed that many illnesses were caused by evil spirits. It may have been the disease itself that was evil. Jesus may have been responding to the perceptions of the people.

In any case, Jesus recognized this woman's need. She did not come forward, nor did she ask anything. She just was there. Jesus called out to her when he saw her, "Woman, you are free from your sickness!"

Then he went over to her, and placed his hands on her, those loving and gentle hands that had healed so many. Immediately she was cured. She straightened up, as she had not been able to do for eighteen years. Her reaction was immediately to praise God. She was cured! What joy she must have felt. Her friends around her were just as pleased. After all these years, an instant cure!

But not everyone was happy. Some onlookers found Jesus' behavior totally out of line. Included in this group was the official of the synagogue, the one who had probably invited or at least allowed Jesus to teach there that day. In his mind, Jesus had committed a crime. He had broken the Sabbath by performing some work, in this case the work of healing.

It is interesting that the angry official did not lash out directly at Jesus. He turned his attention to the people, especially the woman who had been cured.

"There are six days in which we should work. So come during those days and be healed, but not on the Sabbath." If this needy woman had not come on the Sabbath, Jesus would not have broken it.

This official was the kind of man who was afraid to address a strong person, such as Jesus, so he scolded the weak and the poor instead. We are all familiar with this kind of behavior.

But Jesus had no intention of letting this poor woman and others with her be castigated. He defended her and what he had done. Jesus pointed out in bold and forceful language that any one of them would untie an ox or a donkey on the Sabbath and allow it to drink. They would care for their animals and not allow them to suffer even a short time.

"Here," he said, "is this woman, a descendant of Abraham whom Satan has kept in bondage for eighteen years. Should she not be freed from her bonds on the Sabbath?"

Jesus called her a daughter of Abraham to point out that she was one of the chosen people, worth far more than any animal they would care for. Surely she needed to be freed. In this case, Jesus' enemies were ashamed of themselves.

We know that again and again Jesus would be accused of breaking the Sabbath, even though what he usually did was cure on the Sabbath. His accusers were the Pharisees or the Scribes, the more educated people. The simple people had no such problem. What Jesus said made perfect sense to them. Of course, this woman should be freed on the Sabbath. They rejoiced in what Jesus did. They congratulated the woman, and no doubt asked her over and over what it felt like to be cured.

Simple people are frequently the ones whom God finds it easiest to work with. Simplicity is not to be equated with ignorance. Some very well educated people retain simplicity. Simplicity allows one to go directly to the heart of the problem. Simple people do not complicate issues or split hairs. They look for what really matters. In this story, what Jesus did was perfectly right. Of course, even on the Sabbath, God's work is to be done.

One of the problems Jesus continually came up against was the attitude of the Pharisees. They were more concerned with the letter of the law than with the spirit. By their endless study of the law they kept adding to the number of rules they believed a devout Jew should keep. Of course, the ordinary people were thus continually finding themselves inadvertently breaking laws. Additional laws did not draw them to God, but only made the relationship more difficult.

The woman in this story could not worry about breaking the Sabbath with her healing. She was a simple woman, and she knew that he who cured her must surely be of God and that God must approve what he did. There was nothing else to say.

DISCUSSION:

1. *This poor woman had been bent over for eighteen years. We know people today who are afflicted sometimes in like manner. Does God still cure people?*

2. *In this story there is no mention that this woman asked for a cure or even pushed herself forward. Perhaps she was shy or afraid. What do we learn about Jesus from the way he acted here?*

3. *Is the problem of the Pharisees still with us, the problem of people quick to criticize others for their failures in religious behavior? How can we cope with this problem?*

Jesus' Mother and Brothers
Matthew 12:46-50

JESUS was at his work, talking to people, curing them, giving them hope, changing their lives. He was doing what his Father had asked him to do. As he was speaking, his mother and brothers arrived. We know Mary, his mother, of course, but we are not sure what the exact relation of these "brothers" to Jesus was.

No doubt Mary and these relatives came to see Jesus, to visit with him. Mary might have wanted to make sure that everything was all right with him. She might have brought him some food and clothing. She knew very well that he was not likely to be concerned with such things himself.

When they arrived, Jesus was busy talking. They did not want to interrupt. They decided to wait outside. But their presence was noted by others. "What is it you want?" someone may have asked. "We just want to talk to Jesus," Mary or one of the others would have said.

Before long, the message was sent to Jesus. "Look, your mother and brothers are standing outside, and they want to speak to you." Jesus stopped in his speech. We do not know exactly what he was talking about. But he knew how to turn an interruption into an occasion to make a point. Perhaps just as he was interrupted, he was talking about the children of God. When someone mentioned his mother and brothers, he took advantage of the occasion.

"Who is my mother?" he asked, "who are my brothers?" Then he pointed to his disciples and said, "Look, here are my mother and brothers. Those who do the will of my Father are my brother, my sister, and my mother."

And then what happened? Were Mary and the other relatives insulted? Did they feel that they were being neglected? Did they leave that day without even talking to Jesus?

Not at all. Certainly Mary understood Jesus very well. He was accepting into his family all those who accepted his Father's will, the will which his natural family, especially his mother, had long since accepted.

There is a beautiful message here for us. Jesus quite willingly takes us into his family. Mary knew, as we all must realize, that as children grow older they belong to others besides ourselves. Mary realized that day, what she had no doubt known for a long time, that the small intimate family which had lived in Nazareth was over. Her family would now have to include all the followers of her son.

Children grow up, they leave home. All of them, especially those who have a larger mission, will no longer be able to come home and be only ours. Or if they do, they will bring home with them their friends and companions.

This starts very early. Little boys or girls who ask to bring home their little friends are already asking their mother to take in some more children. This is a very healthy thing. No family can be complete in itself. Yet it is always painful when the children move out and the family becomes as large as their world. In this case, Mary had to accept the whole human race.

But Mary was equal to the task. Since whoever does the will of Jesus' Father is his brother and sister and mother, then his mother Mary is doubly his mother. For she, of all people, was the first to accept the will of his Father, that long ago day in Nazareth when she accepted whatever God asked her to do. Each day it became clearer that God was asking her to embrace more and more of the whole world.

DISCUSSION:

1. *Do the words of Jesus to his mother seem harsh in this Scripture passage? How would you respond if your son said these to you?*

2. *How do you picture the scene that immediately followed this incident? Did Jesus sit down and talk with his relatives or did he just move on?*

3. *What was Jesus' purpose in saying what he did?*

The Canaanite Woman
Matthew 15:22-28

THIS woman of Canaan was not a Jew, but a pagan. She believed in many strange gods, no doubt, but they were no help to her. Her daughter had a demon, she said, and was in a terrible condition.

Someone must have told her about Jesus. It is easy to imagine village gossip. "There is a preacher," they told her, "who goes around and cures people." Maybe he will cure my daughter too, she thought, I am going to find him.

She set out on her way. When she got there, she found Jesus surrounded by many people, notably his disciples. She pushed her way through to him. "Help me," she begged. Jesus did not answer. This woman was not in the least discouraged. She cried all the louder.

Jesus and the group moved on. She moved on too, yelling to Jesus. He still ignored her. The disciples were getting a little put out at her yelling. "Send her away," they told Jesus, "she keeps following us and making all this noise." She was certainly not a quiet and retiring kind of person.

Jesus finally responded to her in an even tone, "I was not called to cure pagans. My call is to the lost sheep of Israel." By now this woman was kneeling at his feet. "Help me," she cried, as if to say, help me anyway! My daughter needs you.

Here Jesus was very harsh, it seems. "It isn't right to take the children's food and throw it to the dogs." He as much as called her a dog. What a humiliation. But this woman was beyond humiliation. She was equal to the challenge. "That may be true, sir," she said, "but even the dogs eat the leftovers that fall from the master's table."

Jesus had the answer he wanted. "Woman," he said, "how great is your faith. Your daughter will certainly be cured." And the daughter, still at home, was cured immediately.

What a beautiful story of love and faith. This woman loved her daughter, and would do anything for her sake. If it meant going a long distance, humiliating herself and taking insults, putting up with people (like the apostles) who wanted to send her away, she would bear it.

There are few loves stronger than that of a mother. Mothers will do anything for their children, but this mother was exceptional. No one would call her a weak woman, fainting away in time of trial.

The other remarkable quality of this woman is her faith. She believed that Jesus could cure her daughter. She knew that if he agreed to do so, her daughter would be saved. Coming as she did from Canaan, she certainly had little understanding of the message that Jesus was bringing. But she did understand one thing well: this was no ordinary man. He had power and he would use it for someone who needed help.

In this case it is clear that Jesus wanted her to ask and to keep asking. If she had left immediately after he first ignored her, her daughter would not have been cured. But she had enough faith to keep asking. And certainly enough love to do so.

How marvelous to have Christ himself admire one's faith as he did with this woman. And we today, too, must admire this faith. It can be a true inspiration to us when we ask and ask, and our prayers do not seem to be granted. Perhaps what God wants of us is simply our persistent prayer. He may seem to be ignoring us, as Jesus did in this story, but he is certainly listening. And the day will come when he will answer our prayer.

We do not know the future of this woman or her daughter. We see her only for a brief moment in the Gospel. She was nobody important, so to speak — her name is not even given — but her story has been told for two thousand years, and all because she had two of the world's greatest gifts, faith and love.

DISCUSSION:

1. *Is this woman's love for her daughter unusual? Are her effort for her daughter's welfare unusual?*
2. *What are your reactions to the statement of Jesus that it is not right to give the food of the children to dogs?*
3. *The Gospels constantly stress that faith is the key. Jesus cures because of the faith of those who ask to be cured. What meaning can this have for us?*

The Wife of Zebedee

Matthew 20:20-28

JAMES and John, the two sons of Zebedee, were very close to Jesus. They loved being his disciples. Occasionally they went home to their mother and told her all about it. She was happy to see her sons so happy. The more they told her of Jesus, the more pleased she was that her sons had become his friends.

As she saw it, and as perhaps her sons told her, he was someday going to come into his kingdom. This kingdom would be here on earth, she thought. Perhaps he would be the leader who would drive the Romans out. She was convinced that her sons had found the right leader in their lives.

Mrs. Zebedee, we can call her (since we do not know her name), was, as mothers are, ambitious for her sons. They were such marvelous young men, her mother's eye told her, they deserved to have an important place in his kingdom. Perhaps she told them to ask for the top two positions, or perhaps they told her to put in a word for them. We do not know. When this story is told in Mark 10:35-45, it is the sons themselves who make the request.

In this passage in Matthew, Mrs. Zebedee has come to Jesus himself with her sons to ask. She bowed before him and said that she had a favor to request of him. Jesus looked at her. "What is it you want?" he asked. She answered, "Promise that these two sons of mine will sit at your right and your left when you are king." Any king would need good counselors, she was saying, and these two young men would be just right.

Jesus may have been slightly amused. He knew that her understanding and that of her sons was still very weak as to the nature of his kingdom.

"You do not know what you are asking," he said to her. Then he said to James and John, "Can you drink the cup I am about to drink?" In other words, could they accept all that he would have to accept? He was referring to his sufferings and death, no doubt, but neither Mrs. Zebedee nor James nor John understood that.

They immediately answered that they could. Jesus must have nodded. He knew that eventually they would share his sufferings and death. "You will indeed drink from my cup," he told them, "but I do not have the right to choose those who will sit at my right and my left. These places belong to those for whom the Father has prepared them." His kingdom, he was trying to tell them again and again, was not of this world. Mrs. Zebedee had to be satisfied with this answer. She is not heard from again here. Perhaps then she left.

The other disciples were indignant with James and John that they had asked for the best places and that their mother had been in on it. We know that on other occasions they argued about their positions in the future kingdom. Jesus had to call them together and set them straight. His kingdom would be different. The greatest in his kingdom would be the one who serves. To be great, one must become small. It is a lesson that he tried to inculcate with his own example. He came to serve, he said, not to be served.

This lesson does not yet seem to be well-learned, even by Christians. Perhaps the wife of Zebedee understood it better than her sons did, though. For in this story, she was asking for something for her sons, not for herself. In fact, that is a rather consistent pattern of the women in the Bible. They are doing things for their sons or their daughters.

We do not really know what kind of person Mrs. Zebedee was. She might have been a pushy woman or she might have been one normally shy (if she was like her sons, she was not shy). In any case, in order to do something for her sons, she was willing to overcome her shyness, if necessary, or to face the criticism of others.

She is not held up to us as a model. After all, she misunderstood Jesus' kingdom. But there is a side of her that is quite admirable and that is her mother's attitude, her willingness to make any effort for the sake of her sons.

And thank God mothers are like that. When all else fails, mother will not fail. The love that mothers have for their children is one of the most astonishing and strongest loves in the world.

She may have been mistaken about the kingdom, but she was not mistaken about Jesus. He would listen to her, he would not laugh at her, nor humiliate her. Instead he responded as best her understanding could cope with. A mother's prayer for her sons before the throne of God will not be put aside. God listens to mothers. He has proved that over and over again.

DISCUSSION:

1. Do you think that it was Mrs. Zebedee's idea to come to Jesus with this request, or did the idea originate with James and John? If it originated with James and John, can you relate to this woman?

2. What do you notice in the response of Jesus? Does he show anger or annoyance at this kind of request? Even when we misunderstand God's wishes for us, is he likely to turn our requests aside?

3. When the other apostles were indignant, was it because they were appalled at the misunderstanding of James and John, or was it because they too wanted the top positions? How have women, in a sense, usually been given the privilege of serving, as Jesus said he came to do?

Martha and Mary
Luke 10:38-42

FREQUENTLY Jesus was tired, weary of being on call all day and all night, wanted by everyone, to care, to work miracles, to lay his hands on them. He must also have gotten tired of explaining things to his apostles, who came across at times as rather slow to understand. Whenever he was tired and in the vicinity, Jesus knew a place in Bethany where he could go to rest. It was the home of Martha and Mary and their brother Lazarus. He was always welcome there. Very simply, they loved him. Jesus was a teacher and companion to his apostles, who also loved him. But with Martha, Mary, and Lazarus, Jesus was a friend.

When he came to their house, he could put his feet up and relax. Martha and Mary were always glad to see him. I always imagine that Martha was the older of the two sisters. She would be the one who would be concerned about getting food ready, preparing a good supper for him. One can imagine her as the kind of woman who would chide him for being so thin, for not eating right, for allowing other people to run him ragged. Martha was the kind of woman who took care of other people.

At least on this occasion, she was annoyed with her sister Mary. Mary just sat in the living room with Jesus, at his feet, and talked with him and mostly listened, while Martha did all the work. She was annoyed at Mary and confident enough of Jesus to complain to him. But he defended Mary. This story is usually interpreted to say something about being overly busy. But let us look at some other things too.

First, of all, it is clear that Jesus needed not only good food and rest, but also someone to talk to and listen to him. He liked having Mary there to talk to. She was a non-critical listener, one who accepted what he said and cared about him. Remember that Jesus had his share of critical listeners. The Pharisees, for example, were always just waiting to find fault with everything he said. Or his apostles, who were still struggling with their belief. What a relief it must have been for him to have Mary to talk to. Thus, we can understand Mary's role here. And I think we would all wish to be like Mary, Jesus' own confidante.

But there is a problem in this story about Martha. We might want to be like Mary, but frequently we women are expected to go to the kitchen and do the serving. This even happens at church functions, for example. Now women usually accept this service as a service to the Lord. I think perhaps that Jesus was telling us here that the privilege of listening to him, of sitting at his feet, is a woman's right too.

There is nothing that says it is a woman's place to be always in the kitchen. It is as important, indeed, "the better part" to sit at Jesus' feet and listen to him, as it is to do the more active service.

I imagine that after this little incident, Martha went back to the kitchen and finished up the work. Then she called Jesus and Lazarus and Mary and they all ate together. We know what Jesus was like. We know he must have appreciated Martha's work. And he probably told her so. But I would also like to imagine that the next time Jesus came, Mary took her turn in the kitchen and Martha was able to spend her time with Jesus.

In any case it is clear that women are called also to contemplation as well as to action, called to listen to and savor the words of Christ.

DISCUSSION:

1. *How do you feel about the story of Martha and Mary?*

2. *Does this story tell us that there is something less worthy about the Martha role?*

3. *How can we solve the dilemma of wanting to spend time at Jesus' feet, but wanting also to serve him by serving others?*

Martha and Mary at the Death of Lazarus

John 11:17-44

WE are back again with Martha and Mary. What a beautiful story this is, full of faith, hope, and love.

Before the selection read here, when Lazarus became ill, Martha and Mary had sent a message to Jesus: "Lord, the man you love is ill." So confident they were of Jesus. Yet although Jesus knew how ill Lazarus was, he chose not to come immediately. When he did come, Lazarus was already dead.

Martha, the busy one, as we have seen, when she heard that Jesus was in town, went to him immediately. Mary stayed at home. Martha gently chided Jesus, "Lord, if you had been here, he would not have died. But I know, even now, whatever you ask of the Father will be given."

She didn't really ask Jesus to raise Lazarus from the dead, but almost. When you think of what a tremendous thing it is to raise someone from the dead, this is an audacious thing to say. And remember that Lazarus had already been buried.

Jesus told her that Lazarus would rise again, and Martha made a beautiful act of faith. It is well to remember, at this point, that in the Jewish religion it was not all that clear that there was an afterlife.

Jesus told her even more: "I am the resurrection and the life. If anyone believes in me, even though he dies, he will live." Martha answered that she truly believed that he, Jesus, was the Christ, the Son of God, the Messiah. Now we know that Martha did much more than serve in the kitchen. She had grasped what many philosophers struggle all their lives to find. She believed.

Then she went and called Mary. "He's here," she said, and Mary went to see him immediately. Mary said the same thing to Jesus that Martha had said, "If you had been here, Lazarus would not have died."

Now we come upon one of the most touching of all Gospel passages. Jesus wept. He loved this family, and he loved his friend Lazarus. This was no general, impersonal love. It was a true natural, human love, as well as a divine one. Certainly Jesus raised Lazarus from the dead as a sign to the people of the times and as a sign to us, but also because he loved and cared about Lazarus.

They took Jesus to the tomb. They rolled the stone away. Then Jesus called him forth. What an astonishing thing to have happened. Try to imagine this in modern times. Sometimes it seems we have heard the Gospel stories too often. It would be good for us if we could try to read it all as if for the first time. How great this miracle was! How much Jesus must have loved this family.

This story is full of meaning for us. Like Martha and Mary, we can learn that sometimes Jesus does not respond to our requests immediately. It would have been a great blessing for Jesus to have cured Lazarus before he died, and they would certainly have been grateful. But what a greater miracle to do what he did. Jesus still treats us that way. He might make us wait until the time is right or better or until we are ready to bear an even greater blessing. Or to give us more opportunities for faith and hope.

Both sisters were beloved of Jesus. Even though, as we have seen in the last story, Mary liked to sit at Jesus' feet, it is Martha to whom he tells the message of the resurrection.

He was clearly preparing this family for his own death and resurrection. No doubt they understood what many of their countrymen did not learn. When Jesus was on the cross, his enemies jeered and told him to come down, then they would believe him. They forgot the greater miracle of rising from the dead.

We also learn from this story how great is the gift of love. The members of this family loved each other, and they were able to reach out and pull others into that love. In this story, we see that there were many others here, relatives, friends, townspeople, and probably, the just plain curious.

All of them, because they were there with Martha and Mary's invitation or acceptance, were also part of this great miracle. When we love others, we share with them our faith and love. Because this family loved Jesus, they were able all the more to love other people.

DISCUSSION:

1. *Have you experienced in your own life one time or other God's slowness to answer prayer, only to see later that ultimately it was better not to get an immediate answer?*
2. *How do you feel when you hear of Jesus weeping? We read of Jesus getting angry, of Jesus being tired, and now of Jesus weeping. What image do these give of Jesus?*
3. *Does the house at Bethany where Martha and Mary lived come across to you as a place where you would feel welcome? Why?*

Pilate's Wife
Matthew 27:19

PILATE was having all kinds of problems this day with the Jews concerning a certain Jesus, and in the midst of all this he received a message from his wife: "Have nothing to do with that just man. Today in a dream I suffered much because of him." Pilate sighed and went back to work.

Pilate was a Roman in a strange land. Many times he must have wondered how he happened to get the assignment to be procurator in Judea. There were so many lands ruled by the Romans, so many other countries that the Romans were occupying. Why did he have to get this one?

There were times when he thought that he and the Romans were doing a fine job. Except for not being able to hold the top official positions and having to pay taxes, the occupied people were allowed to continue their old ways. The Romans were even able to make use of local talent, such as Herod, tetrarch of Galilee. They tolerated the Jewish religion, and respected it enough to order that the Roman eagle not be displayed near the temple. To the Jews that would have been idolatry. Further, the Jewish ruling body, the Sanhedrin, was still functioning. This group could decide many of the laws and even judge criminals. They could not, however, execute anyone. A death sentence had to be ratified by Pilate.

He was the procurator, answerable to Rome. His job was to keep the country in order and to keep the taxes coming in. And, as the Romans were good administrators and careful record-keepers, he had to send in written reports frequently.

When Pilate was sent to this outpost, it was no doubt a promotion for him. He may have been pleased with the assignment. Apparently, he chose to take his wife with him. Or perhaps she asked to go with him. Women of wealthy families in Rome lived a rather pampered and free life. They had no real power, but they were able to use their time and talents much as they wished.

We can imagine this wife of Pilate. She may have been bored or she may have been interested in everything she saw in Jerusalem. Maybe she longed to be back in Rome with her friends. Maybe she found the Jewish religion interesting. It seems obvious, however, that she paid attention to what was going on around her. Perhaps she had maids who reported directly to her. Or, perhaps on this day, when she saw all the people in the streets howling for blood, she asked what was going on. Somehow or other, she had heard enough about Jesus, and encountered him in her dream, that she had become convinced he was innocent. And she cared enough about him and about the effects of that innocence on her husband that she sent him a message.

Pilate also knew that Jesus was innocent. He tried to find ways to release Jesus without offending the Jews. Pilate was not really a wicked man. He was simply a weak man, one who allowed himself to punish an innocent man because he was not courageous enough to act on principle.

Did he listen to his wife? Not really. Chances are, though, that he took her dream seriously. It was common in those days to believe in dreams. And the fact that her dream is mentioned at all shows that it must have struck people at that time or later as significant.

Pilate's wife was a pagan. We know nothing about her, not even her name. But we do know this. In her own way, she believed in Jesus' innocence and wanted to save him. She made practically the only defense for him at his trial.

Judas betrayed him, Peter denied him, the other disciples ran away, afraid. Others who had listened to him and seen his miracles now testified against him. Some women followed him and wept. Their witness was not acceptable at the trial. But this woman went straight to her husband with a message. One of the most unfortunate mistakes Pilate ever made was not to listen to his wife. And yet she was only saying what he already knew.

DISCUSSION:

1. *Does it strike you as surprising that Pilate did not listen to his wife's warning?*
2. *Was there anything else Pilate's wife could have done to save Jesus that day?*
3. *What do you think of the fact that only Pilate's wife, a pagan woman, spoke up for Jesus' innocence that day at the trial?*

Women Whom Jesus Meets on the Way to Calvary
Luke 23:27-31

A large crowd of people followed Jesus as he carried his cross on the way to Calvary.

Some of these were his enemies. They were gloating over their victory and glad to see that he would now die. Perhaps they went along to be sure that nothing happened on the way to intervene, that nothing would keep Jesus from dying. After all, they were aware of miracles that he had worked. What if he worked another miracle now?

Some of those following Jesus were his friends, those who had been with him on his journeys, or who had witnessed his miracles and had come to believe that he was no ordinary man. We know that his disciples, with the exception of John, did not stay close to him on this terrible walk through Jerusalem. But there were unnamed others who were there, especially women.

Some people in the crowd were simply curious. Jesus was not the first person to be led through the streets of Jerusalem carrying a cross on the way to his death. There had been many others and there would be many more. These people came to watch any condemned criminal being executed. Some people are interested in watching any tragic scene. On this day, the number of the curious was probably much greater than usual. They had heard that this man had worked miracles, made the lame to walk, the blind to see, even raised the dead to life. He had preached to crowds of people and challenged the Pharisees. His crucifixion might be interesting, they thought, and so they went along.

We do not know to which of these groups the women of Jerusalem mentioned in this Scripture passage belonged. Some of them may have been his friends or had perhaps heard him speak. Some had started out by being curious and were now overwhelmed with pity for him. What we know is that these women, when the crowd was screaming for his blood, felt compassion for him. Perhaps they saw his mother weeping and identified with her. What would it be like if this were their son? In any case, they felt sorry for him.

Jesus noticed them. He turned and spoke to them. Jesus was notably silent on his way to Calvary, speaking only a very few times. When he did speak, then, it was important to listen to what he had to say.

He told them not to weep for him. He was doing what his Father had asked of him. They should not weep for his sufferings; they should weep for what may befall them in the future. It seems he was saying that compassion should not be misplaced. He did not need their pity. He needed that people would turn to God, that they would avoid the causes of the suffering to come.

We know that pity and compassion are not necessarily feminine qualities. The society in which we live has not always allowed men to show such feelings. But women have been expected to give vent to their natural feelings of compassion. This natural compassion, this ability to sympathize, to identify with the suffering person is of great value. But, as Jesus pointed out to these women, pity in itself is useless unless it is translated into action. We must not only feel for others, but we must do what we can to help them.

It should also be of great inspiration to us that Jesus spoke to these women on his way to Calvary. In the midst of his great sufferings, he chose to talk to these women, to give them a final message. He spoke of their needs, not of his own. Jesus was a man for others until the end.

DISCUSSION:

1. *What do you think of these women of Jerusalem meeting Jesus on his way of the cross? How do you picture them? How do you think they responded after Jesus spoke to them?*

2. *Are there times we feel we should close our hearts to the natural pity we feel for someone, because we are afraid of being drawn into a difficult situation? Can you think of examples? How can we solve this dilemma?*

3. *Is weeping a feminine and/or childish way of responding to a situation? Does it serve any useful purpose?*

Women at the Cross
John 19:24-27

IT is significant that this story is from John's Gospel. What happened at this time, John would never forget.

Jesus was hanging on the cross dying in greatest agony. Guards were there; their duty was to make sure that the sentence of execution was carried to completion. No one would be allowed to prevent the death of this notorious criminal.

No doubt, some of these soldiers had served at executions before. One of their privileges was that they were allowed to have whatever the criminal still had at the end. There was rarely much of value. Usually, as in this case, there was simply his clothes.

This criminal seemed to have one item that was not easily divided. It was a seamless robe, made of one piece of woven cloth. Right now it might have been blood-stained, but even the rough Roman soldiers could see that this was a good robe and once it was washed it would be all right. They decided not to cut it, but to cast dice to see who would get the robe.

Mary, Jesus' mother, was there while all this was going on. Chances are it was she who wove the robe for him. She may have watched the soldiers gambling for it. But who had the robe interested her very little. What did matter to her was that her son was dying there on the cross.

She stood at the foot of the cross. Her sister was there too, identified here as Mary, wife of Clopas. No doubt this is again a cousin (a family would not have named two daughters both Mary). Another Mary was there too, Mary Magdalene, whose love for Jesus was uncrushable, no matter what happened.

There was only one disciple there, John. He had followed all the way, but — he would have been the first to admit — not courageously. At least, however, at the end, he stood openly at the cross.

Jesus was dying in agony above these people. He looked down at his mother and at John. "Woman," he said to his mother, "here is your son." And to John he said, "Here is your mother."

This may well have been a symbolic giving of his mother to all of us, but on the surface level, it was Jesus' way of providing for Mary. We know how precarious was the existence of widows in Israel, especially widows who had lost their sons. In fact, Jesus himself raised the son of the widow of Nain just for this reason. By now Mary must have been a widow, for we hear no more of Joseph.

Jesus, although he was dying in the greatest suffering, still thought of others. He was concerned about his mother. He wanted her to be provided for, and so he asked John to do it. John's response may have been nothing more than a nod of his head, for no oral response is given here. But after Jesus' death, he did take Mary into his home as Jesus had asked.

Christians for centuries have contemplated Mary standing at the foot of the cross. She stood, we are told; she did not swoon or faint away. She stood there bravely with full acceptance of God's will, in accordance with the way she had accepted his will from the first moment when she was told of his coming.

She stayed with Jesus to the end. She would not leave. In this she showed herself a true mother. Others may leave and reject a person, but a true mother will support her son no matter what. In many other circumstances one has to prove oneself. One does not need to prove anything to a mother. A mother is always a mother.

Mary is that kind of mother to us too. Sometimes, in today's modern world, we forget Mary's motherhood. All of us need a mother through all our lives. We never reach the point when we no longer need that kind of support and caring. And Mary is always there looking out for us, standing there for us.

Other women were at the cross: Mary's cousin, the wife of Clopas and Mary Magdalene. We are not surprised to see Mary Magdalene there; by now we know how much she loved Jesus and how she would brave any crowd to be with him. The wife of Clopas is not mentioned by name elsewhere in the Scriptures, though it is likely that she was part of the crowd of women who followed Jesus and ministered to him. She may have been one of the women who were among the first to be told of the Resurrection. If so, it is truly fitting. It is very like Jesus to allow these women who sorrowed with him to the last to be among the first to rejoice. Women can be proud of their record in the last dark days of Jesus.

These women had simple faith and simple love. They were not concerned with what the crowd might think, or say, or do. Would that today we had that kind of simplicity.

DISCUSSION:

1. *Imagine yourself standing near Mary and the others at the foot of the cross. What would you say to Mary, if anything? Or is there something she would say to you?*

2. *Do you see any significance in the fact that the seamless garment was not to be torn?*

3. *What can you say about the way Jesus arranged for his mother as he hung dying?*

Women at the Resurrection

Matthew 28:1-9

THE Sabbath was over at last, with its enforced rest. Jesus had died in agony on Friday. To some of the women who loved Jesus, that Friday had been an incomparable tragedy. But they had no time to contemplate the tragedy. Even Pilate understood the sacredness of the Sabbath for the Jews. The body was taken down hurriedly before the sun set. It was laid in a tomb, one that a wealthy benefactor, Joseph of Arimathea, had provided. It had all been done hurriedly, with people rushing to complete the task before sundown.

During the day of Sabbath when all work was forbidden, Jesus' women followers fretted. Jesus at least deserved to be properly buried. His sacred body should be wrapped in spices to preserve it somewhat longer from corruption. They could do nothing on the Sabbath but they would take care of that unfinished business as soon as they could, very early on the next morning. And so these women who loved Jesus, including Mary Magdalene, Mary the mother of James, and Salome, went to the tomb with spices.

Most women can identify with them. A task is not over until it is done properly. And one of the tasks that frequently falls to women is taking care of the personal needs of others. Women do this for their children, all the clothing and bathing and feeding and soothing that children need. They do it for their husbands; they do it for others. Here too, these women who most likely had cared for Jesus during life by providing food or washing his clothes, now wanted to care for his dead and wounded body. It would give them comfort

to know that, although they could not prevent his crucifixion, they could at least offer a measure of dignity after
death.

But Jesus had much greater things in store for them. As
they approached the tomb, they started to wonder. Who will
roll the stone away for us? They must have known that Pilate
had set guards to prevent any of Jesus' disciples from steal-
ing the body away. Certainly they didn't think they would
get any help from the guards to move the stone. They did
what women tend to do: they planned the service they could
perform, and then figured that the rest would take care of
itself one way or another.

And it did. When they arrived at the tomb, according to
Matthew, there was a strong earthquake and an angel from
heaven came down and moved the stone. He sat on it. The
women must have stared in awe at him, sitting there in
blinding white garments. The guards trembled with fright
and apparently fainted.

Not so the women. They had come to find Jesus and
even an angel would not deter them. What a contrast here
between the women and the Roman guards. There is something here about the simplicity of the weak with their faith in
God and their devotion to a task that the strong of this world
will never understand.

The angel spoke: "I know you seek Jesus. He is not
here. He is risen as he said. Come in and see the place where
he had been laid."

These women, in spite of their great love and faith in
Jesus, had failed to grasp that message. Jesus had said he
would rise again. Even the Pharisees remembered that, as
they asked Pilate for a guard for the tomb. But Jesus forgave
these women that lapse of faith. They were the first to
receive the message of his Resurrection. Women have

always had to bear the disgrace of being daughters of Eve, tempted to sin in the garden. Now they have the honor of being associated with the ones who stood at the cross with Jesus to the end and of being the first to be informed of the glorious Resurrection.

The women were then told to go and tell the disciples. What joy these women must have felt. It must have seemed to them that suddenly everything fell into place. Jesus' death had not been an unrelieved source of sorrow. His death had been what he had come into the world for. But it was over now. He had won that victory. He had risen from the dead and he would die no more.

They hurried back to tell the disciples, who had been even more despondent than they had been. Of course, the disciples were skeptical at first. These were hysterical women who were probably imagining things. But the disciples loved Jesus too much not to find out for themselves, and so they rushed to the tomb.

How loving of Jesus to send an angel to inform these women and have them relay the message to the disciples. It was the usual touch of Jesus. He seemed always to prefer the little and the weak, those that the world would overlook. The testimony of women was not even valid in court among the Jews, but Jesus used women for this great testimony. These were simple women, concerned with simple things, like service and work. Jesus chose them to give the world's greatest message: he is alive and lives forever.

DISCUSSION:

1. What are your thoughts as you watch these women going to the tomb in the early morning because they want to embalm Jesus' body properly? Is there a connection here between humble service and the opportunity to be a witness to God's message?

2. *Do you think it bothered the women that the apostles were skeptical when they arrived with their marvelous message that Jesus had risen from the dead?*

3. *Does it strike you as strange that the Pharisees remembered that Jesus said he would rise again, whereas his closest disciples and friends seemed to have overlooked that?*

Mary Magdalene at the Resurrection

John 20:11-18

MARY Magdalene went to the tomb. She had been with Jesus to the end, and now she wanted to make sure that in death his body would receive proper care. Mary Magdalene loved Jesus. Once she became his follower, she never left him.

These last days had been painful ones for her as she watched him be arrested by his own people, turned over to the Romans, judged to be innocent and yet condemned to die. And she knew he was dead. She had seen him die on the cross.

Even now, though, she did not want to leave him. When she arrived at the tomb, she saw that the stone was rolled away. She ran to Simon Peter and John and told them, "They have taken him away and I don't know where they have laid him." The two disciples ran and found the empty tomb.

Mary Magdalene came back too. She was weeping because she had lost Jesus completely. Even his body had been taken away.

She looked into the tomb and saw two angels. They spoke to her, "Woman, why are you weeping?" Isn't it astonishing that Mary saw two angels and showed no surprise at seeing them? Not even angels from heaven could console her if she did not have Jesus. She turned away from the angels.

Then she saw someone else standing there. Through her tears, she thought he must be the gardener. Maybe he was the one who had removed Jesus' body. She said to him, "If you have taken him away, tell me where you have put him. I will go and get him."

Did she imagine that she would be able to lift the dead weight of his body? But Mary Magdalene is not a practical woman. She is simply a loving woman.

Jesus then said, "Mary!" And she immediately recognized him. What joy must have filled her at that moment. Here he was, alive!

Mary then did the most natural and likely thing. She reached out to him, she touched him, she wanted to hold on to him forever, that he might never again die or go away. But he would not allow that now.

No, he said, do not hold onto me now. He went on to tell her about his Ascension. Soon he would be going to heaven. As for now, she was to go and tell the disciples.

From what we have seen of Jesus throughout the Gospels, this story does not surprise us. This is exactly how we have known the loving Jesus to act. For those who love him, he is always there. Jesus would not leave someone who chose to be always at his side.

There are other familiar touches of Jesus, such as the fact that he was not present immediately. We have seen Jesus act this way before. It is as if he wants us to seek him. He loves us and wants to be with us, but he knows that the efforts on our part to seek him will make him all the more welcome when he comes. And when he does come, he may be in disguise. Here Mary did not recognize him immediately, but mistook him for the gardener. We know how often Jesus comes to us in disguise too. He told us why. When we receive others in his name, we receive him.

But Jesus' disguise is quickly put aside. Here he speaks only her name, Mary, and she immediately knows him. On another occasion in these deliriously happy days after Easter, the disciples recognized him as he broke bread at table.

There are ways to recognize Jesus. They seem to be geared to the needs of each person. Many of us are like Mary Magdalene. When Jesus speaks our name, we know him. We are like the sheep that the Good Shepherd knows by name.

Jesus still speaks to us. To those who love him, he draws near and calls their name. We know that he loves us as much as he did the Jews of two thousand years ago. We, like Magdalene, cannot cling to him physically. His reference to the Ascension called attention to the fact that the physical phase of his life was over. He would now live another life, a resurrected one in which he would not be found by space and time and physical necessities. As the resurrected Lord, he can be present to all of us as he was to Magdalene on that first glorious Easter.

DISCUSSION:

1. *Can you picture Mary Magdalene in this story, as she went to the tomb, saw angels and other wonders, but was not at all interested, because she was searching only for Jesus? Is there a message here for us?*

2. *Give examples, if you can, of times in life today, when Jesus comes to us in disguise. In what ways does he reveal his presence?*

3. *This scene is filled with joyous excitement at the fact of the Resurrection. The final message of the Gospel is one of joy. As Christians should be known by their love, should they also be known by their joy? Does this seem true in the Church today?*

Women as Part of the Embryo Church

Acts 1:12-14

JESUS lived, Jesus died, Jesus rose from the dead. For forty exhilarating days Jesus stayed with his people, teaching them all the things he still needed to make clear to them before he would leave. However, he assured his people, as he still assures us, that he would always be with us. He would send his Holy Spirit who would guide the Church. The Church, his people themselves, would need to take his place on earth, giving his message and his mercy to all.

Then the day came when Jesus went up to heaven. His closest friends and disciples watched him go. One era of God's working was over and a new one was about to begin.

Still, the transition was difficult. After all that Jesus had taught, the disciples still felt like helpless children, as indeed they were. After Jesus ascended into heaven, they stood there, looking up. Two angels came and told them to go.

So they went back to Jerusalem to the upper rooms where they had been staying. Besides the apostles, the Scriptures also mention that women were there, including by name Mary, the mother of Jesus.

Women were there from the very beginning. At no time in the whole Christian message were women excluded. Christianity is not a male religion. When anything is happening, women are there. Women were always a part of the close followers of Jesus. Mary was the first believer and retained that position. She did not head the Church, but she was the prime believer.

Further, the influence of the women was vital. Christianity taught a message of concern for the poor and the weak and those whom the world despised. Jesus said repeatedly that he would not choose people the way the world did. His message was one of serving, not being served. Nor had he done less himself.

Women are frequently excluded from the power circles of the world. But in the Church of Jesus, where the values of the world are turned upside down, women will be there. They will follow the example of Mary and the other women who spent time in prayer with the disciples. Whatever is going on, they will be there.

A few days later, when the day of Pentecost arrived, all of the believers were gathered together. Certainly at least half of these believers must have been women, the same women who had followed Jesus during his life and witnessed his death. When the Holy Spirit came, he came for the women as well as the men. They, all of them, were filled with the Holy Spirit and began to speak in other languages. This gift of tongues was given to all whom God chose.

Human beings make distinctions among persons; God never does. He chooses whom he will. It is very like him to choose the weak and those whom the world despises.

There is a powerful message here. When the strong despise the weak, they are not acting the way God would have us act. When persons are excluded for any reason, we need to think carefully. Our restrictions may not be of God. His power reaches out to all, especially to the weak.

God is as active as he ever was in the Church today, giving his gifts to men and to women, to the gifted, wealthy, and powerful, as well as to the ignorant, the poor, and the weak. It is up to us to see to it that his gifts are recognized wherever they are, in whomever they reside. God may speak to us in a bag lady as well as in the most exalted bishop.

Whatever else can be said about women's rights and women's liberation, one thing is certain: God may choose whom he wishes to do his work, and he does precisely that.

DISCUSSION:

1. *Women were a vital part of the Church from the very beginning, even immediately after the Ascension of Jesus. Is there a message here for us today?*

2. *Can you think of special events in the life of the Church when God chose the most unusual persons, particularly women, to do the things his Church needed doing?*

3. *What kinds of things do you think the first women in the Church did? What kinds of ministries did they perform?*

Ananias and Sapphira
Acts 5:1-11

THE women whom Jesus met were usually alone. We hear of certain women who were the wives of this person or that, but we do not see them as couples. However, in the early Church, couples abound. Ananias and Sapphira are one of the many couples who joined the first followers of Jesus.

We also see in Acts the sense of a community of believers that began to be developed. As long as Jesus was with the disciples, they looked to him for guidance. Now they found that they needed to pray together for guidance from the Holy Spirit. Jesus had said that he would send his Spirit. And he did. The Acts of the Apostles have been called the Gospel of the Holy Spirit.

The first Christians were not only a community of believers, but, according to this passage, they also shared their belongings. In this way, they all contributed to the group and were able to help anyone in need.

Here, then, we have the situation. Ananias and Sapphira had some property which they decided to sell and give the proceeds to the group. But, for one reason or another, they decided not to give it all. Their faith and trust were not yet deep enough.

Ananias went first with the money to Peter. But Peter, enlightened by the Holy Spirit, knew what he had done. His sin was not keeping back the money. After all, it was not required that everyone turn over all he had to the group, as Peter here says. But why did he lie? One must not lie to the

Holy Spirit. When Peter found him out, Ananias fell dead. All the people standing around were filled with fear, as well they might be.

Then Sapphira arrived. Peter questioned her about the money and she repeated the lie that she had agreed on with her husband. Peter asked her why she too lied to the Holy Spirit, and then told her what had happened to her husband. At that, she too fell dead. All the others were filled with great fear, we are told again.

This does seem excessive. However, we are not told that it was a punishment. It may have been a response to their own guilt and fear. We do not know enough details. Certainly, it must have been clear to all those there that the power of the Holy Spirit was alive in the early Church.

Can it be said that Ananias led Sapphira into sin, that she did what he asked, even though it was a lie? We do not know that, but it is possible. It is also possible that it was Sapphira who convinced her husband to hold back some of the money.

The relationship between husband and wife is a very powerful one. It can be even stronger than that between parents and children. The marriage relationship is entered into voluntarily and at an age when one is mature enough to make a choice. And, for better or worse, the married partners profoundly influence each other's lives.

Most people marry, and a marriage is usually the basis of their entire life outside their work. That is why a good marriage is so important, and why no success in any other field can compensate for a failure at home. Persons, men or women, who sacrifice their home life for the sake of their work, make a big mistake. Ultimately, their work suffers too. The deep and strong foundation will be lacking.

It would be hard to overestimate the influence that any woman has on the life of her man. It can be the opposite also. In this story, Sapphira lost her life along with her husband because she agreed with him to lie. When he went down, she went with him.

We know nothing about this woman except this present story. It is certainly a sad one. We would not expect Sapphira to come into Peter's presence and contradict her husband. Even today in civil courts, wives are not asked to testify against their husbands. But perhaps at home at the very beginning, Sapphira could have changed Ananias' mind. She could have told him not to do what he did. Women are much more powerful than they realize. In a loving marriage, a woman can make her man the kind of person he was meant to be.

DISCUSSION:

1. *Does this story leave you frightened, as it apparently did the first Christians? Is fear the message of the story?*

2. *Why do you think Sapphira and Ananias agreed on this deed? What could they have done differently?*

3. *What are your feelings about the power of a wife in a family?*

Tabitha

Acts 9:36-42

TABITHA was an early Christian who was characterized by two qualities: a deep and abiding faith and an outgoing charity. She spent all her time, we are told, doing good and helping the poor.

She was an excellent example of the types of people the Holy Spirit produced. As Paul said, some were given the gift of preaching, some of teaching, some this gift, some that. Her gift was that of kindness and service to the poor, especially toward the widows.

She must have been a skilled seamstress, making and giving clothes to the widows. We know the precarious life of widows in the first century, how little money they had for food, not to speak of clothing.

When Tabitha died, the widows stood around her holding the cloaks and other items that she had made for them. No doubt she did not just give them serviceable garments, but went the extra mile and made clothing that was beautiful. Perhaps she did some small embroidery on them. Tabitha is the example of the woman who served others, but did it with love and enthusiasm.

Yet she fell sick and died. Her body was laid out and her friends, the widows and others, came to mourn her. She must have been held in high esteem in her town of Joppa. Peter at that time was in Lydda, not far away, and when the disciples heard he was there, they sent two men to him. They asked him to come immediately. People cared about Tabitha.

Peter knew her too, and came as soon as he got the message. When he got there, he found the scene of mourning. The beloved Tabitha was dead.

Peter had learned well from the Master. He, as Christ had done, put the mourners from the room. Then he turned to the Heavenly Father and prayed. Perhaps he was unsure how to proceed. Yet, after his prayer he was strengthened.

He arose, turned to the dead woman and said, "Tabitha, get up!" Immediately, she opened her eyes, looked at Peter, and sat up. Peter reached over and helped her from the bed.

We do not know what they said to each other. Perhaps nothing. What was there to say in the presence of such an astounding miracle?

Peter called the disciples and especially the widows, and presented Tabitha to them. They were all amazed and filled with praise for God. The news spread around and many new persons believed in the Lord, we are told. This is the only instance of anyone being raised from the dead by one of the early disciples.

Tabitha, then, was a believing and holy woman. She was noted for her charity to others, especially widows. We do not meet women like her in the life of Christ. There we meet many women who are completely devoted to Jesus himself, like those who followed him around the country. We meet others who come to him, burdened with sin and asking for forgiveness. But here we meet the results of Jesus' coming. Tabitha understood what he meant when he said that what was done for others was done for him. She served Christ in serving others.

Today some people are wondering whether or not such personal services are still viable. Maybe professional organizations should take care of the poor. And yet we have all seen what happens then: charity quickly becomes a bureaucracy in which the individuals are lost.

Tabitha would not have forgotten the individual. We can imagine her sewing, making garments for her widow friends. She would have been well aware of them as people. No doubt she personalized her work.

Tabitha does not seem to have been a widow herself. Yet we hear nothing about her husband here. Perhaps he was not yet a believer. Perhaps he didn't believe he had time for the things Tabitha devoted herself too. Yet it is strange that he is not mentioned at all at the time of her death. For this story it is not important. Tabitha was the giver, the respected follower of Christ. Whatever the circumstances of her personal life, it was for her own qualities that she was esteemed.

DISCUSSION:

1. *There is a tendency today to speak with derision of "do-gooders." Perhaps some would have called Tabitha one too. How would you respond to that?*

2. *Do you see anything particularly feminine in the type of giving that Tabitha chose to do? Is there a lesson here for us?*

3. *What do you make of the fact that the only raising from the dead performed by a disciple of Jesus was this one of Tabitha?*

Lydia
Acts 16:11-15

THE first Macedonian city in which Paul stopped was Philippi. There he did what he always did in new cities. He waited until the Sabbath and then went to the synagogue so that he could preach about the Messiah who had come to fulfill the longings of the Jews.

But in Philippi there were few Jews and no synagogue. The Jews who were there met in a temporary place of prayer. When Paul arrived that Sabbath, he found only women. Apparently the Jewish men in that city were not numerous or devout. So Paul spoke to the women. Among them was one who paid very close attention to what he said. Her name was Lydia.

We can imagine Lydia as she listened. As Paul spoke, we are told, God touched her heart. She believed in the message that Paul gave. After the others left, Lydia no doubt remained behind. She wanted to hear more of Paul's message of Jesus. As they talked, Paul learned some things about her too. She was a sort of business woman, engaged in dying purple cloth. Apparently she was successful and quite wealthy.

We do not hear of her husband, and she is not called a widow. This may mean that she was single, perhaps still young and unmarried. Or perhaps she was married, but her husband was involved in other things and other religions. We do not know. We do know that, as far as the Christian community in Philippi was concerned, Lydia was a leader.

After several discussions and many visits of Paul to her home, Lydia and her whole household were baptized. Then she invited Paul and his companions to stay with her during their days in Philippi. After much urging from her, they agreed to do so.

Later, as the days went by in Philippi, Paul and Silas got in some trouble with the townspeople. They had exorcised an evil spirit from a girl, thereby causing her master to lose a rather substantial income from her fortune-telling. Paul and Silas were beaten and thrown into prison. But God rescued them and helped them to convert their guard. They knew then that it was time for them to move on from Philippi. Before they left, however, they stopped at Lydia's house and spoke to all the believers there, all those who had so recently been converted. Her house thus became the first official Christian community gathering place for the town.

It is interesting that this woman was the first to be called by God in this town and that she apparently presided over the first Christian community here. Paul, who has been accused of being sexist, did not seem to find this a problem. He was quite impressed with Lydia and convinced that her call was from God.

There are many women today, as there were in the past, like Lydia. She was an energetic and strong woman. She was also, before Paul's coming, a devout Jew, open to God's word. She was ready to receive God's message through Paul.

Lydia ran a large and wealthy household. Her commerce, the dying of purple cloth, was the kind that put her in touch with other wealthy people. Purple was the stuff of kings. She was identified by her business, not as someone's wife or mother, although she may well have been both. She was an important and influential woman in the city. Paul no doubt recognized that her house was the ideal place to center the community. Being wealthy, she was one of the few people in town who had a house large enough for the people to gather and for Paul to preach.

After her conversion, there is no indication that she stopped being a business woman. No doubt she continued her business, while providing for the Christian community now under her direction.

We know how Christ loved and cared for the poor. There are times when we forget that he also cared for and loved the rich. They too are needed in the Church. Neither they nor the poor are complete in themselves. It is not the financial state of the person that is important, but the person himself or herself. As Christ reached out to the rich and poor, so did Paul. When Christ touched the hearts of the rich, they often showed it by their concern for the poor.

Perhaps Lydia was already much concerned with the

poor in her city. We know that she was a devout woman. But with the coming of the Christian message, she had an added incentive; Christ told us that what was done for others was done for him.

DISCUSSION:

1. *What message can you learn from the fact that Lydia was apparently a rather wealthy and independent business woman, and the person most ready for the message of Jesus?*

2. *Do you think that Lydia presided over the prayer sessions that the first groups of Christians in Philippi held when they met at her house?*

3. *Do you imagine that there were any changes in Lydia's dedication to her business interests after she became a Christian?*

Priscilla and Aquila

Acts 18:24-26

HERE we have another couple, another husband and wife who were together involved in the early Church. Yet how different they are from Ananias and Sapphira, who had not really given their hearts to God.

This couple had lived in Rome. They had had to leave because the emperor Claudius had ordered all Jews out of the city. So they went to Corinth. When Paul arrived in Corinth he heard about them, went to see them, and stayed with them awhile. One can imagine why. Paul made it clear that he was a Roman citizen. People in the city must have told him that there were some Romans here and directed him to Priscilla and Aquila's house.

Paul worked on tent-making in Corinth, earning his own living. One can imagine him also spending many hours telling Aquila and Priscilla the story of how Jesus had spoken to him and changed his whole life. Priscilla and Aquila must have felt greatly honored to have Paul stay with them.

When Paul left Corinth, after many days, he set out for Syria, and he took with him his dearest friends, Priscilla and Aquila. When they arrived in Ephesus, Priscilla and Aquila stayed there. Apparently, by now Paul thought them sufficiently grounded in the message of Christ that they could be his ambassadors. He himself moved on and went to Jerusalem and other areas.

Back in Ephesus, a certain man, a Jew named Apollos arrived. He was an excellent speaker and had many things to say to the people of Ephesus, as he spoke in the synagogue. However, his knowledge was incomplete. He knew the message of John the Baptist, but had not apparently heard of Jesus. Perhaps he had left Israel before Jesus came on the scene.

In any case, Aquila and Priscilla listened carefully to him. They recognized his piety and sincerity. All he needed, they knew, was further instruction. They invited him to their home and told him how Christ had come to fulfill all the prophecies of the Old Testament and how John the Baptist was only the precursor of Christ. They spoke so eloquently and so movingly of Jesus that Apollos was converted. Then he moved on to Greece. As he went, Aquila and Priscilla wrote to their relatives and friends in Greece, asking them to accept him.

Aquila and Priscilla could be called one of the first

missionary couples. They are always spoken of together. There is no indication that only Aquila preached and Priscilla did other works. It seems that they operated as a team. When they traveled, they traveled together. When they preached, they preached together.

Their background indicates that they were well-educated and well-traveled. They had lived in Rome, Corinth and Ephesus. They were familiar with the best culture of the day. They saw what Rome was like at its height, and what Greece was like after its golden age. Through these years, they were devout Jews.

After they met Paul, they became devout Christians and they were the ideal couple to be missionaries. With their non-provincial background, they were able easily to adapt to new customs and new people. Also, it is likely that they spoke several languages.

Couples like Aquila and Priscilla can form the backbone of a church. Such a couple, who share their deep and abiding personal love, and who are able to share their faith and missionary zeal, are an invincible entity. What they set out to do will be accomplished.

Perhaps there are too many occasions in which there are special church services and organizations for women and others for men. There are, of course, Cana Conferences in preparation for marriage, and Marriage Encounters for the married, but these focus on the marriage itself. What may be needed are more opportunities for married couples to work together on church functions. After all, marriage itself needs to be seen as the source of great spiritual strength.

How fortunate Aquila and Priscilla were to have found each other, both dedicated to the same concerns. And they were able to make good use of their wealth, independence and education. They were able to devote themselves to their work, knowing that they had each other for support. In a good marriage, nothing is more supporting than the other person.

Finally, it seems clear that Priscilla was one of the first women to preach. Paul accepted her along with her husband. He was wise enough in the Lord to recognize the strength of their marriage and the need they had of each other's support.

DISCUSSION:

1. *Why is it that there are few married couples in the Catholic Church who devote themselves as a couple to service? Why are there so few couple-oriented opportunities in the Church, outside of those concerned with marriage itself?*

2. *How do you picture this couple? What kind of woman do you think Priscilla was?*

3. *Would Aquila have been less effective in his work without Priscilla? Do marriage partners sometimes hamper each other?*

Paul's Women Friends and Benefactors

Romans 16:1-16

OF all Paul's letters, the one to the Romans was the longest. Rome was a city he intended to visit, but never did, until he was brought there as a prisoner, and martyred there. At the end of this long letter, there is attached a series of greetings to many people, including a number of women. It is clear from lists and references such as this that women formed a large and important part of the early Church communities.

The first person to be mentioned is Phoebe. She had been active in the church at Cenchrea, serving the people of God and Paul personally. Some have called her a deaconess, involved not only in feeding and clothing the poor, but also in advising, counseling, and consoling. Paul spoke highly of her and asked the community to receive her in his name. No doubt she was a strong woman, a leader in the community.

He mentions the missionary couple Priscilla and Aquila. They had saved his life, Paul says, and deserved everyone's thanks and respect. It is very likely that Phoebe would have stayed with them in Rome when she arrived. We know well that a loving couple always has room for one more, especially one who is so obviously a sister in the Lord.

Paul mentions Epaenetus who has the distinction of being the first in the province of Asia to believe in Christ. Then he mentions Mary who, he says, has worked so hard for them. What precisely she did, we do not know, but in the early Church, the two works were always serving the poor and preaching the Good News. She may have done some of both.

Further down the list of persons are Rufus and his mother, as well as Nereus and his sister. These two women are not mentioned by name. Perhaps Paul did not know them so well, but no doubt their work was just as dedicated or important for the Church.

What we learn from this list is quite obvious: Paul had met and converted many women in his early missionary travels. There is no evidence that he ever thought of women converts as less important than the men. In addition, many of these women were outstanding in their communities, and performed significant work for the early Church. These were strong women who had to face the kinds of problems all the early converts had to face, ridicule, persecution, and perhaps even death. They did not shrink from such involvement. Paul, led as he was by the Spirit of God, never rejected any of these women nor downplayed their gifts. He knew well that whatever they were inspired to do was from the Holy Spirit.

The Holy Spirit today calls women as much as he has ever done. This is very obvious in all the churches. As men are called to serve God, so are women. There has never been a time in the Church when there were no holy women, never a time when women have not performed heroically for the Lord.

Today the Holy Spirit is again speaking to women. The world has changed and the needs of individuals have changed. But there are some needs that go on as long as there are human beings: the need for food and shelter, the need for counseling, consoling, and just plain listening. Women today, like Phoebe and the others at the time of Paul, will always be needed for these occupations in the Church. Just how women will put into practice the ministries the Spirit calls them to may not be clear at the beginning. But it is certain that the same Spirit who calls women will help them see the opportunities in which they may use their gifts.

DISCUSSION:

1. *Does it surprise you that women played such a large part in the leadership in the early Church? Does Paul appear to be sexist?*

2. *How do you think the community at Rome received Phoebe when she was sent by Paul? What do you imagine that she did in Rome as she settled in?*

3. *What seems to you to be the call of the Holy Spirit to women today in the Church?*

Marriage and Virginity
1 Corinthians 7:1-7

PAUL is here responding to questions that apparently were raised by the faithful in Corinth. Some must have asked him about marriage. No doubt they had many concerns about such things. Corinth had a reputation as a very licentious city. John McKenzie, the Scripture scholar, says that the two industries of Corinth in those days were shipping and prostitution.

Paul was well aware of the temptations of his fledgling Christian community in a city where it was as common for a man to stop in at a brothel after work as it is today for men to stop in at bars. The people in Corinth saw this as something quite natural and normal.

But Paul told the Christians they were called to something higher. Now, what about marriage? Some of the Corinthians must have asked. Is this not also a sexual relationship? Since sex can be such a problem, would one not be better off never marrying?

We must remember that it was a very novel idea in those days to choose never to marry. The Jews, for example, had no particular use for celibacy. As far as they were concerned everyone should eventually marry.

Paul says that yes, it would be well not to marry. But since human beings seem to have so much trouble with chastity, marriage is the solution for most people. Let a man have his own wife and a woman her husband. They should fulfill each other's needs. Note here the equal rights of marriage as portrayed by Paul. The man must not see his body as his own, but belonging to the wife, and the woman must not see her body as her own, but as belonging to the husband. They should provide for each other's needs, and here, it is clear, that Paul means sexual needs.

He also says that they should not abstain from sex, unless they have agreed to ahead of time, and then only in order to spend time in prayer, and then only for a time.

Paul is neither anti-sexual nor is he unrealistic. He is aware of the temptations and needs of human beings. When he says that he would like to see others live as he does, unmarried, he makes it clear that this is a particular gift, but it is no greater than any other gift is. He had in mind that the second coming of Christ would be very soon and that people should remain as they are and not make major changes in their lives. Instead they should devote themselves to living well in whatever state they are in, in order to prepare for the coming of Christ.

For a long time in the Church, there was an unspoken understanding that somehow the vocation of marriage was a second-class one, that marriage with its important component of sex, was somehow only a concession to weakness. Further, it was thought that somehow in a marriage, the husband was considered the person with the needs and the wife was to be ready to service him when he asked. How all this came about is certainly not obvious from Paul. He makes it clear that some persons have one gift and others another, and that marriage is for the needs of both partners.

What we can learn today from this passage? Certainly we can appreciate Paul's message of the fact that marriage is good for people, that most people need marriage, that it is not a second-class calling. It too is a gift. Most women today are married, most women want to be married. In spite of the fact that the call of marriage is a call to self-sacrifice, a call to devotion to husband and children, most women choose to be married. There are many joys of marriage, especially the joy of sharing one's life and love with another very special person. Later the two will share that same joy and love with children. But joy and love are not incompatible with suffering and pain. They are the usual parts of a marriage too.

Women who are called to virginity, or perhaps, after the death of a husband, to the life of widowhood (which was honored in the early Church), are also given a special gift. These women have perhaps greater opportunities to devote themselves to others outside the home. Many married women must give most of their time and effort to their own children and homes. Together, though, the married and the unmarried women can give strength and support to one another. They can work together as sisters. Fortunately today in parishes this has begun to happen. Religious sisters and married women are involved in many things together. Paul would have been pleased.

DISCUSSION:

1. *Do you recall sermons on vocations in your childhood in which it seemed that the only "vocation" was to the religious life?*

2. *What benefits do you think married women and the unmar-ried, the single, the divorced, as well as religious sisters, can derive from working together?*

3. *Can you think of models in the early Church or among the saints who exemplified holy married women?*

Respect and Love in the Home
Ephesians 5:21-33

ST. PAUL had a message for husbands and wives. Submit yourselves to one another, he says, because of your reverence for Christ. The word "submit" had quite a different meaning in those days than it did today. It certainly did not imply that one person subjected the other to all kinds of whims and demands. In any case, St. Paul says that they are to submit to one another.

Then he goes on to say that wives especially are to submit themselves to their husbands, as to Christ. Husbands, he says, have authority over their wives. Now, this passage may seem irksome to many modern women. They see it as saying that it is the privilege of men in a marriage to demand some kind of obedience of their wives.

Paul was, of course, writing from his own culture. He had never seen a marriage in which there was any kind of equality or equal sharing of responsibilities. Now if women always found themselves being subjected to a husband (who, as likely as not, was not even chosen by them), what better way to cope with their circumstances than to look to Christ and his Church for a model of behavior.

Paul was not making a new law which was to last for all time. He also said, in another place, that slaves were to obey their masters. He did not thus say that slavery was to continue forever. We have seen that Paul did not see a need of any drastic social change. He was convinced that the Second Coming of Christ was imminent.

What is more significant about this whole passage, and what has strangely been neglected in many sermons on it, is Paul's much more lengthy instructions to husbands to love their wives. As women did not choose their husbands, neither did men choose their wives. Frequently they were matched up with someone who would unite the families for business or other reasons. Yet Paul instructs them to love their wives. He does not say anything like, "Husbands, command your wives, or lead them, or order their lives." Instead he tells them to love their wives, after the manner in which Christ loves his Church, even giving his life for his Church. That is a very high example of love. How strange that in the centuries since Paul spoke, this passage has not been made more of.

Marriage, then, according to Paul, is not to be like marriage among the pagans around them in which men often treated their wives as little better than slaves, and women resented and sometimes hated their oppressive husbands. The Christian marriage was to be one of love and respect. A marriage in which both husband and wife love each other is the only kind of marriage worthy of the name.

We all know that marriage today is in trouble. The statistics on divorce are not encouraging. Very rapidly, it seems, we will reach the time when more than one half of all marriages end in divorce. The causes for this are many and cannot here be considered in detail, but it seems clear that one reason is simply that people no longer make a true commitment to each other when they marry. Paul would have recommended that the married couple make the effort to stay together and to work out their problems long before the problems have become insoluble.

Let us return to the image that Paul makes of a marriage. A good marriage, he says, is like the union of Christ and his Church. Of course, Christ is always faithful to his Church, completely sacrificing himself for it. But the Church is not always so faithful. It is a sinful Church, forever in need of forgiveness. Paul was trying to show that in a good marriage, both partners need to follow the model of Christ and the Church: both should be willing to give and forgive. Certainly it is not the exclusive responsibility of the husband to follow Christ's example. Both must make the effort, as through the years they struggle to make their marriage ever better.

DISCUSSION:

1. *How would you describe a marriage which is lived after the example of Christ and his Church, the model that Paul gives to us?*

2. *Do you believe that this passage has perhaps been misread and misused in the Catholic Church and in other Christian churches?*

3. *Do you think Paul today would write differently about the relations between husband and wife?*

Decorum in Service

1 Corinthians 11:2-16

WHAT a troublesome passage this is! And yet it need not be when understood in the light of the message Paul came to bring, which is Christ's own message.

First of all, it is clear that Paul is speaking to the problems of a particular community, that of Corinth. As we have seen, this city was known its licentiousness, especially its large population of prostitutes. Apparently these women wandered the streets with shaven heads or uncovered hair. Thus Paul wants the women of the Christian community to keep their heads covered, so as to make it clear that they are not prostitutes.

It is to be noted that through many centuries it was the custom for women to wear something on their heads whenever they dressed up. Until rather recently in the United States, for example, a woman was not dressed up unless she wore a hat. When that custom changed for women in secular society, it eventually changed for women in church. Today women do not wear any head coverings in church, and nobody is much concerned about it.

In contrast to the women, the early Christian men in Paul's day changed the Jewish custom of covering one's head when speaking of God, a custom that still prevails among Orthodox Jews. Early Christian men kept their heads uncovered, showing their dignity and authority, Paul says.

He made it clear throughout this whole discourse that he was speaking of custom. At the end he adds that he doesn't want to argue about the issue. It is just a custom and seems to work all right, so he would prefer that people leave well enough alone.

What disturbs modern women is that Paul seems to indicate that women need a head covering because they are under the authority of men, as men are under the authority of God. He says that men were not made for women, but women for men, no doubt referring to the story of Adam and Eve. Paul softens his message a few verses later. In the Lord, he says, woman is not independent of man, nor is man independent of woman. For as woman is made from man, the famous rib, so is man born from woman. And it is God himself who brings everything into existence.

Paul is not making new rules about how men and women should relate, nor especially how they should act in the assembly. Rather he is referring to customs and abuses of those customs that have crept in. He wants there to be a certain decorum, and the decorum for women was to have a head covering.

When Paul is read in his entirety, he is far less sexist than he seems on the surface, or from isolated passages. It is interesting, however, how frequently the part of this passage which points out the authority of men over women is used as God's word, while neglecting the part that neither men nor women are independent of each other.

Paul was trying to come to terms with male and female relations. One cannot make a case from this passage that men are to dominate women. Paul does not want any kind of domination. We know how active women were in the churches Paul worked with, and how much leadership they assumed. Surely Paul did not see those women as less Christian because of their roles in the churches.

This is not an attempt to explain away these passages. Just as Paul was trying to come to terms with what he saw of the world and what he knew of God's call to people, both male and female, so too we must try to come to terms with it.

What then can we learn from this passage? That women should wear veils? Hardly. That women must be under the authority of men? Not likely. Rather, it seems that the major message is that men and women are not independent of each other. We need each other, we need to work together. No man who treats a woman as second class can call himself a Christian. Nor can any woman who despises men do so. Rather, we need to work together for God's kingdom.

DISCUSSION:

1. *Do you feel that this passage has often been used unfairly? If so, why then did the Church so easily do away with the rule that women should be veiled (or wear a hat) at Mass.*

2. *Does it seem to you that women were freer and more a part of the leadership of the early Church than they were for centuries in the Middle Ages and beyond? What might have been the causes for the loss of freedom for women?*

3. *Give your impressions of Paul.*

Women in the Assembly

1 Timothy 2:9-15

THIS is the famous passage of how women should behave themselves in church.

Now, as we know, many of the things in Paul's epistles

were written in response to questions or abuses. Paul here is apparently concerned with abuses in the behavior of some women in the assembly. What he was doing was not establishing new rules so much as re-ordering old rules.

He didn't want women to be over-adorned. That was not proper for prayer in the assembly. One was to come for prayer and to share the word of God, not to show off one's attire. A woman's adornment (and a man's too) should be virtue. Few would argue with this.

He goes on. Women are to be silent in the assembly. They should be submissive and under the direction of their men. After all, he says, it was not man who was deceived by woman. So all women are to be forever punished? This is from the same Paul who says elsewhere that it was through a man that we were led into sin.

But it is useless to argue such things. What was happening here was a discussion concerning order in the churches and apparently some abuses on the part of some women. Women had usually been silent in the synagogues. So there was little familiarity with women as assembly leaders.

Down through the centuries and even now, these lines have been used to keep women from speaking from the pulpit and even taking an active part in church services. In some Fundamentalist churches, the rules are even stricter. And yet it is unfair to Paul to use passages like this to bolster an individual's own prejudices and chauvinism.

The Catholic Church today is slowly changing. Women are doing some of the readings and distributing Holy Communion. Yet, it is not that most women want to be heard in the churches. In mixed groups, women speak up much less than men do. It has been shown by psychological studies that women in groups tend to be silent. In fact when they speak up, they are frequently not listened to by men, or are interrupted.

However, Paul's comment that if a woman doesn't understand something she should ask her husband at home is perhaps, in a certain sense, a useful one. Frequently it is the woman who brings up things at home to discuss. Women are much more likely to talk about religion at home or elsewhere, and it is good for men that women do ask questions at home.

Finally, Paul says that women will be saved through child-bearing. Is this the same Paul who said that he thought it would be better if everyone was as he was — unmarried? How then did he expect unmarried women to be saved?

If Paul were here and we could ask him, of course he would not say that every woman had to have children if she wanted to be saved. What he was referring to was that line from Genesis, the punishment that man and woman each received for their sin. The woman was to have to suffer from child-bearing and the man through the sweat of his brow.

Never does Paul say that woman is inferior or that man is intellectually or morally superior. He knew well that just because some leaders in the Church or society are in positions of authority, they are not therefore superior.

It is a misreading of the Scriptures to use passages such as these to discriminate against women. The God who calls all to freedom and who always respects the whole person does not decide that some persons are superior just because they are male. Paul knew too much about human nature to believe that either.

DISCUSSION:

1. *Have you ever heard this passage used in order to discriminate against women or any particular group of women?*

2. *What would Paul say if he came into our churches today?*

3. *In almost any church, there are more active women members than there are men. As women assume more leadership functions, will the number of active men increase or decrease?*

Widows
1 Timothy 5:3-16

ALTHOUGH in any year, more boy babies are born than girl babies, there always tend to be more women than men in the world. This has to do with the higher mortality rate of the male. Men are more likely to be killed in accidents and wars. Even men who are allowed to have a natural span of life are likely to die younger than women. So it is common today, as it apparently was at the time of Paul, for there to be many more widows than widowers.

The instruction here seems, first, to be directed at families to take care of their widows. The children and grandchildren of a widow should look after her and see to it that she is well provided for.

Then Paul goes on to say that true widows are those who have no one to care for them, but place their trust in God. He is especially concerned with older widows, those who are above sixty years of age.

There was established by this time a sort of order of widows — of women who were older, had been married only once, and who apparently banded together for mutual help and for prayer.

There are a few problems with this passage. One is, it seems, the suggestion that a second marriage was not quite right. Another is the harsh way that young widows are spoken of. Although Paul does not find second marriages edifying, he recommends that younger widows remarry as soon as they can. Otherwise, they will spend their time in gossip and other non-edifying occupations.

Why such lack of compassion for the young women, one may ask. Here, as we have seen before, there may have been abuses among this or that Christian community. One can imagine the young widow who may or may not have young children. It is unreasonable to expect that she would simply devote herself to prayer for the rest of her life, at a time when she needed much more than mere alms from her fellow Christians. For these young women, a second marriage was recommended.

Most people were not meant to live alone. Both men and women are more happy married, if this is their calling. The older widow, over sixty, who is unlikely to have an opportunity for a second marriage, should stay unmarried. Her calling at that point seems to be clear: now she should use her widowhood as an opportunity to grow in the life of the spirit. But the younger widow's vocation to the calling of marriage is still there, no doubt. As soon as is respectable, she should choose another husband so that she may live out her vocation.

The world today does not lack widows. In fact, there are large numbers of widows in places such as retirement villages and the like. When these groups get together for parties and social events, the number of widows often exceeds the number of widowers by about ten to one. Many of these older women are lonely. They may have been well-provided for by their husbands, and their children may be attentive and caring. But their children have lives of their own and these women know well that material needs are not the only ones.

Older widows today can take a lesson from this message to Timothy. Now that their chances of remarriage are low, they might want to look at a second calling. They now have the time for prayer and good works. Some women have found their widowhood an opportunity for new interests and new challenges.

It is no accident that some of the most active women in churches are widows who are devoting themselves to good works. They are present each morning at Mass, they take part in Scripture studies, they are there when there is any service to the needy to be performed. These women also get together with other widows and enjoy each other's companionship and sharing of memories and pictures of grandchildren. Such women have not formed a religious order or community, but they are certainly living a type of sisterhood.

And for others who are not widows, what message? Certainly, we all need to care for widows. They are part of our whole family, part of the group to which we belong. We cannot ever leave them out. Our churches must not make them uncomfortable or made to feel unwelcome. Our widows can be a source of strength for our Christian community. They have much to give and much to share.

DISCUSSION:

1. *Does the fact that widowhood is not a chosen calling make it somehow less worthy?*

2. *What has been your experience of the way widows in the Church have been treated? What kinds of contributions to the community and to the Church do widows make?*

3. *What are your comments about Paul's remarks about the activities of younger widows?*

Older and Younger Women

Titus 2:1-6

HERE is another instruction from Paul concerning men and women. Older men and women are to live unblemished lives so that they can instruct and give example to the younger men and women.

It is clear that Paul is pointing out specific abuses of his times: the references to slander and to overuse of wine are clearly not generally the faults of only older women. As for younger women, he sees them in relation to marriage. His advice to them is to love and cherish their husbands and children, to obey their husbands, to be self-controlled and pure, and to be good housewives. As a rule, he did not envision them in other roles besides these.

What are we to make of these words of advice? For one thing, young women and older women need each other's support. There must not be two separate societies, one for the young and one for the old, or one for men and one for women.

It has been said that women do not relate well to other women. The ancient philosophers did not even believe that women were capable of true friendship with each other! It has been said that women are jealous and back-biting with each other, quick to cut each other down, in order to win the attention of men.

As long as women define their personal worth only in relation to men (whoever attracts the richest or the most handsome or the most successful man is the winner) we may have this kind of competition. But when women see themselves as full persons in their own right, where each one can develop her own capabilities, then we will find women working together. All the love and care that women so naturally give to husbands and children, they are quite capable of sharing and giving to each other as they work together in service.

Women today are forming various kinds of support groups. They need opportunities to share their feelings, their concerns, their experiences. Here is where older women can be so valuable for younger women, showing them compassion and understanding and a sharing of the joys of life. The younger women can also help the older women. They can listen to them, show them they are still valuable, give them the kind of respect that society at large rarely accords to them. Women can work together to make their lives happier.

There is much that younger women can learn from older women. They can learn how to age gracefully, how to handle the problems that come with age. Aging can be more painful for women than it is for men, because when women lose their youth and beauty, they feel they have lost their value. But that is true only among women who have placed their value in such things. A woman is a whole person and her value is there no matter how she looks.

From the older woman the younger woman can learn true beauty, the graciousness and kindness that come from understanding and caring. She can learn compassion and endurance. She can learn that there is no value in not forgiving, no value in not giving and no value in giving up.

The older woman can learn from the younger woman too. She can learn not to hang on to the past, that the present is all any of us have, that the world today still needs her care and concern.

Psychological studies show that women are usually the ones that people talk to and expect to be listeners. Men talk to women, other women talk to women, and children always talk to women. How important listening is today in the busy world we live in, in which everyone seems to be running off in every direction. People need a listener. What a treasure is the woman who has made her home or her heart the place where others are welcome to come and know that they will be listened to.

Paul mentions for both men and women the need for self-control. Self-control is what enables people to persevere, to keep on going, to not allow the small things of life to encroach on the big and important things. But self-control must never interfere with joyous enthusiasm in living, the kind of joyousness that people working together should manifest. Above all else, support groups of older and younger members of a parish should be joyous ones.

DISCUSSION:

1. *Have you found that in many circumstances older members of a group are not paid as much attention to, or considered as important as younger members?*

2. *Why are there sometimes problems between older and younger members of a group? What can be done about such problems?*

3. *What valuable lessons have you personally learned from older members, or younger members, of the community?*

Women and Men in Marriage
1 Peter 3:1-7

HERE we find Peter urging men and women to find a way to love harmoniously in marriage. In the midst of his discourse, he has much to say about women's adornment. Apparently, there were many abuses along these lines. Today perhaps we cannot appreciate how different the early Christians were expected to be from their neighbors, the pagans, who were inclined toward frivolous and vain adornments.

Peter says that a woman's adornment should be the true inner spirit, the ageless beauty of a gentle and quiet spirit which will shine like jewels. Now he had in mind that this was the way a woman could win over her husband who might not be a believer. She need not say a thing. The holiness of her life and her gentleness of spirit would show him the value of the Christian life.

Even in today's world, this concept is worth pondering. We have all been more impressed at times by the holiness of a person's life than by his preaching. Mother Teresa of Calcutta speaks and writes little. Her life is her preaching, and who knows how many have begun to believe in the Christian message because of what she is. Very often, people are turned away from the truth because of the poor example on the part of so-called believers.

Beauty of character is a true adornment. No matter how plain a person is, if he or she is kind and gentle, we see him or her as attractive. Not every man is handsome nor every woman pretty, but all can be beautiful.

Love transforms people. We know well that when we love someone, that person becomes beautiful in our eyes. It works both ways. When someone is in love, he or she is tranformed. Love brings a glow to the skin and a shine to the eyes. The lover needs no other adornment.

Peter goes on with his lesson about how women should respect and obey their husbands while men should love their wives and remember they are the weaker sex, yet called also to God's gift of life. We have already commented on the fact that this kind of advice reflects the world as the writers of the epistles knew it then. Peter gives the example of the holy wife of Abraham, Sarah, who obeyed her husband and called him lord. If Sarah did this, must we then all do it? Peter was here looking for an example of a holy woman. He was trying to fit a woman's role into the world as he knew it.

But the emphasis should not be on the woman's submission so much as it should be on the respect that both husbands and wives should give each other. If husbands truly respected their wives, the whole idea of submission would change. To us today it sounds as if women were to be treated as second-class, as perhaps servants of their husbands, living in obedience. That cannot be the meaning of the respect that husbands were to accord their wives, knowing that they too were called to the life of the spirit.

Married women today do not call their husbands "lord." And husbands have been learning what Peter may well have been trying to tell them: when they love and respect their wives, their lives become truly the lives of kings. They will reign in their wives' minds and hearts. No true man wants a woman who grovels at his feet. What he wants is someone equal to him who truly chooses him as her love match. Marriage must be a meeting of mutual love and respect, or it cannot survive in today's world.

Whenever, throughout the epistles, the apostles give lessons, they are meant for all. All of the lessons of love and humility and faith and compassion that are expressed so eloquently in the Scriptures are meant for both men and women. As all are called to be Christians, so all are asked to share in the full life of the Christian. The few passages that mention women cannot be the only lessons that one reads. Rather, what is said in those contexts must be read in the light of the whole.

Whatever else can be said, it is clear that both men and women are called to be holy and humble and gentle and loving and respectful of one another.

DISCUSSION:

1. *What do you think of the idea that a woman who lives a life of gentleness and kindness will win over her husband? Have you seen this happen?*

2. *Does Peter condemn adornment in this passage? Some groups have understood passages such as this as forbidding all adornment.*

3. *Are marriages happier when women act as obedient children to their husbands?*